Lee vs. Pickett
Two Divided By War

by Richard F. Selcer

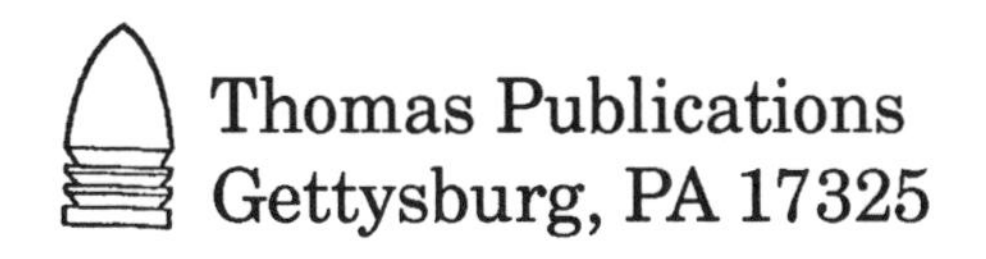

Publisher — Cataloging-in-Publication Data
Selcer, Richard, F.
Lee vs Pickett: two divided by war / Richard F. Selcer
144 pp. 15.25 x 22.9 cm.
Includes index, bibliography.
ISBN 1-57747-030-3
1. Confederate States of America—History. 2. United States—History—Civil War, 1861-65—biography, Confederate. 3. Lee, Robert Edward, 1807-1870. 4. Pickett, George Edward 1825-1875. I. Title
E467.1 .L4 .S4645 923.573 LCC 98-84332

Printed and bound in the United States of America

Published by THOMAS PUBLICATIONS
P.O. Box 3031
Gettysburg, Pa. 17325

Cover design by Ryan C. Stouch

Dedication

This is dedicated to the ones I love:
Janet Lee and Mike—my California "fan club."
Lois, Mother, and Bill—my Fort Worth "support group."

Table of Contents

Acknowledgments

No author ever writes a book entirely solo. There are always countless helpers and contributors who get him down the road little by little. At the time each one is seen as a priceless benefactor to whom the would-be author swears eternal gratitude, but as time goes by their names and contributions tend to blur together. "Acknowledgments" pages like this are the author fraternity's token "thank you" to the small army of foot soldiers who make us the generals of the literary field. Many hands make the work go faster, and many minds help to get it right. Unlike the novelist who usually labors alone, the historian is dependent on his (usually unpaid) army of librarians, archivists, genealogists, proofreaders, resident experts, and colleagues to reach his objective.

Even a slim volume like this one is the product of many hands and minds. The following acknowledgments are not meant to be comprehensive nor exclusive, but simply to recognize some of the more notable contributors along the way. Eternal thanks to Peggy and Bill Nelson and to Lois Biege who are uncredited partners in everything I write. I couldn't possibly sell enough books to ever pay them what they are worth. To Dr. Bud Robertson of Virginia Tech, thanks for originally getting me turned on to George Pickett and Robert E. Lee at your annual Civil War Institutes, and for inspiring me to climb literary heights I might never have tackled otherwise. To Mike Vouri, Gary Gallagher, Wayne Motts, and Bob Krick, thanks for reading early versions of the manuscript, pointing me toward additional sources and tipping me off to dumb mistakes and faulty reasoning. You watched this manuscript grow from a 30-page weakling to a robust 150-page heavy-weight. You helped to whip it into shape along the way. It takes a lot of time to read and comment on manuscripts, even when the subject is near and dear to your heart, and there is no professional obligation to do so except out of kindness or pity!

And to Wayne Motts of Gettysburg, a special thanks for sending me to Thomas Publications where this manuscript found a home after outgrowing the limitations of a journal article. To the librarians and photo archivists at the Virginia Historical Society, the Museum of the Confederacy, the Library of Congress, the U.S. Military Academy, and the U.S. Army Military History Institute, thanks for their expert assistance, both on the phone and in person. Though I may be only one of dozens of research inquiries they receive every day, they are my "A-team." Thanks to William Hopkins of Richmond, Virginia, who has devoted, and continues to devote, countless hours to researching some of the more obscure aspects of George Pickett's life. He has become "My Man in Richmond." To Mike Musick at the National Archives in Washington, thanks for adding me to his list of "approved clients" for whom the Archive staff have frequently come up with that rare document or impossible-to-find primary source needed to fill in some research gap. The day Mike finally retires, a lot of Civil War researchers will go into mourning—or shock! To Darryl Beauchamp at Navarro College, who with the help of a gracious benefactor, has established a new premier Civil War collection right here in the heart of Texas: thanks for opening up the Pearce Collection on odd days and at odd hours and for alerting me to new acquisitions that brought me charging down to Corsicana, Texas, with stars in my eyes. Thanks to Dr. Gabor Boritt of Gettysburg College for his moral support and professional encouragement. I still hope to be a "head-liner" on a C.W.I. program some day! Thanks to Jacque Hopkins for providing homemade cookies and hours of proofreading. Finally, to Dean Thomas for taking in a homeless manuscript in 1996, and Sarah Rodgers, my editor at Thomas Publications, who served as midwife to this book, a great big *muchas gracias*!

And to anyone I have left out, my profoundest apologies. I'll try to do better on the next book!

LEE VS. PICKETT
Two Divided By War

1 Inquiring Minds Wanted to Know

In 1904 as he approached the end of a full life, eighty-two-year-old former Confederate general Eppa Hunton sat down to dictate his reminiscences to his son. The old soldier spoke freely, with unguarded frankness, because most of his comrades from the Civil War were dead, and besides, he intended his recollections to be seen by only his "immediate family and a few intimate friends." Recalling the last days of the war when the Army of Northern Virginia was dying a slow, painful death, he interrupted the narrative to muse about two Confederate legends he had known well: "General Pickett had lost cast[e] entirely with General Lee [although] I cannot tell exactly what the trouble was."[1]

Another old Confederate general, John S. Mosby, writing in 1911, was also intrigued by the relationship between Robert E. Lee and George Pickett. But his comments were made in a national magazine, reopening old wounds and stirring up a hornet's nest. He noted that Lee "didn't like" Pickett, and as for the object of that dislike, "I was very slightly acquainted with Pickett and know nothing of his differences with General Lee."[2]

These two old campaigners were the only Confederate veterans ever to comment for the record on a problematical relationship quite apparent to observers during the Civil War—namely, the bad blood between Lee and Pickett. Otherwise a code of silence seemed to be thrown over the relationship by all concerned. John B. Jones, a clerk in the Confederate War Department during the war, wrote in his diary in 1864, following the latest in a series of clashes between the two officers, "It is possible that General P[ickett] may have on some occasion criticized Lee."[3] But Jones was as much in the dark as everyone else about the root cause of the apparent feud.

Library of Congress, Washington, D.C.

U.S. Army Military History Institute, Carlisle, PA.

The two most resolute debunkers of the Pickett Myth, as they appeared after the war, Eppa Hunton and John Mosby. Both outlived most of the Lost Cause mythmakers and were shrewd observers of their fellow war heroes.

George Pickett and Robert E. Lee were never personal friends, contrary to later claims by Mrs. Pickett, so it cannot be said that there was ever a break in their relationship. That relationship was always formal and strictly professional, but it was rocky nonetheless. It included a series of poor performance reviews of Pickett, a returned after-action report, and some mysterious orders dismissing Pickett from the Army of Northern Virginia just before the curtain rang down at Appomattox. All of which begs the questions, what exactly was the problem between the two men and what was the nature of their relationship. Unfortunately, the close-knit fraternity of Confederate officers and the protectiveness of their early biographers have prevented the Lee-Pickett relationship from being fully investigated. Helen Dortch Longstreet, the second wife of General James Longstreet, was merely perpetuating a cherished myth of the Lost Cause when she wrote that Pickett was "one of Lee's favorite officers."[4] She was not in a position to know since she only met "Old Peter" and married him late in his life, after both Pickett and Lee were dead.

The second Mrs. Longstreet never knew either Lee or Pickett, but she did understand the importance of preserving the myth of the Lost Cause, and she did her part for the Cause the same as many other former Confederates and their widows.

But instead of accepting Helen Longstreet's sentimental moonshine, we need to look for the relationship in the official records and the memoirs of the men who knew both principals. There is unfortunately little direct testimony, but there are strong hints of unresolved issues and much circumstantial evidence, all pointing toward the same conclusion: Robert E. Lee and George Pickett intensely disliked each other.

Modern scholars who have spent years studying the Civil War in general and the high command in particular have been as perplexed by the Lee-Pickett relationship as their contemporaries were. Glenn Tucker, one of the deans of Civil War historiography, in *Lee and Longstreet at Gettysburg* observed that, "There was no necessity and there appears to have been no justice in [Lee's] break with [Pickett] in the closing stages of the war."[5]

2 Two Gentlemen of Virginia

On the surface, these two gentlemen of Virginia had much in common, including the trivial matter of sharing the same middle name, Edward. Both grew up on the fringes of the proud Tidewater aristocracy and were products of the United States Military Academy. At an early age, both assimilated the code of the Southern gentleman, which demanded "courtesy, deference to women, hospitality to strangers, defense of his honor, [and] consideration for social inferiors."[1] On Lee the mantle of aristocracy fit comfortably whereas George Pickett was never at ease among the Southern blue bloods, constantly having to prove to himself and others that he belonged.

Lee was eighteen years older than Pickett, and his family circumstances had forced him to take on adult responsibilities at a young age. Pickett grew up in a sheltered environment where tragedy and disappointment did not intrude. Both young men inherited a strong martial heritage with the family name which helped to push them toward their chosen careers. Robert Edward was the son of Revolutionary War hero Henry "Lighthorse Harry" Lee, but apart from his military exploits, Henry Lee was a poor role model for his son. He was brave enough but never possessed the requisite self-discipline to achieve lasting success. The flamboyant elder Lee, after first drinking himself into debt and shame, abandoned his family when Robert was only six. Henry Lee fled to the West Indies where he died when Robert was eleven. Thus Robert never had a strong father figure in his life. He got his sense of duty and selfless service from his mother, and in adulthood those were the same qualities he admired most in others. Lee made an almost obsessive effort all his life to be the man his father never was—steadfast, devoted, dutiful. In command of the Army of Northern Virginia, he became the stern "father" to his military family.

George Pickett's father Robert was a gentleman farmer, not a soldier. He was active in affairs of the Episcopal church and local politics, but contributed little to the family legend of "the Fighting Picketts of Fauquier County," a proud tradition going back to the French and Indian conflict of the previous century. The elder Pickett was a good provider and a loving father to his three children, but as a parent he was rather indulgent of his oldest son. The strongest influence in George's life while growing up was his mother. It was her desire that he become a lawyer like his Uncle Andrew Johnson, but when George proved unsuited for a life of books and jurisprudence, she gave her blessing to his decision to enter West Point.

West Point, which Lee entered the same year Pickett came into the world, was a defining time in both men's lives though hardly in the same way. They were only two among the 303 West Point alumni who fought for the Confederacy in the Civil War, but that fact alone does not begin to tell the story.[2] The Lee and Pickett legends actually begin at West Point. The exclusively male society of the Academy and the heavy emphasis on discipline brought out the best in Lee. Pickett resented the regimented lifestyle and demanding routines, preferring boyish pranks to serious studies. Lee at the end of four years ranked second in his class (1829) and equally important as a measure of character, did not have even a single demerit on his record. He was cadet sergeant his second year and adjutant of the corps his third year. Those who knew only the soldierly side of Lee found his no-nonsense demeanor quite intimidating; those who breached his frosty reserve discovered a man of profound sympathy and kindness. But all admitted that his mere presence commanded respect even as a cadet.

Pickett, on the other hand, ranked dead last in his class academically at graduation (1846) and had accumulated close to 199 demerits in four years, the maximum number allowed before automatic expulsion. He constantly thumbed his nose at the rules, refused to apply himself in the classroom, and struck everyone as unlikely officer material.

Lee came through West Point with superb marks and the profound respect of all who knew him, but without the firm, fast friendships that were such an important part of the West Point

U.S. Army Military History Institute, Carlisle, PA.

The United States Military Academy as painted by George Catlin in 1828, one year before Robert E. Lee graduated. West Point did not look so very different when George Pickett first saw it in 1846.

experience for most men. Pickett, by contrast, impressed no one with his soldierly qualities, but made a number of valuable friendships that were instrumental in his later career. Among those he formed a bond with were James Longstreet (class of '42), Ulysses Grant (class of '43), George McClellan and Cadmus Wilcox (both, class of '46).

Lee's performance as a student ultimately won him an appointment to the exalted engineering corps upon graduation while Pickett's left him no other option but the lowly infantry. Only the fortuitous outbreak of a major international conflict in 1846 kept alive any hopes he had of a future career in the military.

War is a soldier's *raison d'etre*, his fast track up the promotion ladder, and the bigger the war the greater the opportunity. The Mexican War presented both Lee and Pickett with an opportunity to shine. Lee was a forty-year-old captain with no previous field service; Pickett, a twenty-one-year-old, shave-tail lieutenant fresh out of the Academy; neither of them were going anywhere in the peacetime army. Each caught the eye of his superiors, performed heroically in battle, and won multiple brevets—that is, honorary rank bestowed on the spot for gallant or meritorious action, but not (yet) confirmed by the War Department. During the course of fighting in Mexico, Pickett won two brevets, and Lee, three.

Lee's ultimate rise to army commander really began when he joined the staff of Winfield Scott in January 1847. Demonstrating the value of a mentor, it was Lee's endorsement by the keen-eyed Scott that got him positioned for subsequent choice assignments.

Lee learned something else in the Mexican War besides how to conduct himself under combat conditions. Scott's army was full of ambitious, egocentric officers, jockeying for promotion and glory. They spent almost as much time fighting with each other as fighting with the Mexicans, often appealing over Scott's head to political allies back in Washington. Eventually the in-fighting caused Scott to be recalled, much to Captain Lee's mortification. Watching this bickering and back-stabbing, Lee wrote his brother Sidney Smith Lee deploring the situation: "The dissensions in camp have clouded a bright campaign.... To suspend a successful general in command of an army in the heart of an enemy's country; to try the judge in place of the accused, is to upset all discipline; to jeopardize the safety of the army and the honor of the country, and to violate justice."[3] Lee saw first-hand what internal dissension could do to an army, how it could eat away at leadership and morale. For Lee, discipline, justice, and honor were the bedrock of military success, and they must never be compromised. He vowed that if he were ever at the head of his own army he would do everything in his power to ensure harmony and cooperation among his officers. The only redeeming factor in the Scott imbroglio was that by the time it came to a head, the enemy was defeated and the army had won its objective. How much worse might it have been if all of the squabbling had occurred at a critical point in the campaign, when the army was deep in enemy country and needed every soldier to do his duty, Lee shuddered to think.

Stuck in Mexico City when the war ended, Lee joined most of his brother officers from the Regular Army in forming the Aztec Club, a fraternal military order that would link the participating veterans for the rest of their lives. For unknown reasons, Pickett chose to remain aloof from the organization despite the fact that practically every other Regular Army officer joined.

After the Mexican War, Lee went on to a series of staff assignments, reflecting once again the high regard in which he was held. Captain Lee returned to West Point in 1852 for a three-year tour as superintendent. As he did in every other endeavor, he applied himself assiduously to being the best superintendent he could possibly be. To the cadets he always displayed sympathy and respect, treating them as though they were his sons. When some of his "sons" proved unable to make the grade at the Academy, he thoughtfully allowed them to resign rather than suffer the embarrassment of dismissal. The end result was the same but it saved everyone's feelings and preserved their dignity. Superintendent Lee was harshest on those who were closest to him, including his own nephew Fitzhugh Lee, whom he tried to dismiss for a drinking incident. Lee could be kindly but he was never soft-hearted. Duty and discipline were the standards he set for himself and everyone around him. Appointed Lieutenant Colonel of the Second U.S. Cavalry on March 3, 1855, Lee was posted to Texas, but he spent little time there in the next five years.

Lieutenant George Pickett remained in line duty, however, going with his regiment to Texas. Then, in 1855, the same year Lee arrived in Texas, he was transferred to the newly created 9th Infantry Regiment organizing at Fort Monroe, Virginia. He received his long-awaited promotion to captain in the Regular Army on the same date Lee was promoted to lieutenant colonel, March 3, 1855. The Ninth was posted to Washington Territory where Pickett again found fame and controversy in equal measures. He seemed to be a man always in the middle of history-making events, though never in control of those events.

Neither Lee nor Pickett was actively involved in the sectional crisis of the 1850s, though both owned slaves and opposed the tyranny of the Federal government. Lee might have been speaking for both when he wrote in early 1861, "If the Union is dissolved, I shall return to Virginia & share the fortune of my people."[4] Neither man doubted the right of secession, which, as Pickett pointed out, "was taught in our text-books at West Point." Both cherished the Stars and Stripes and all that it stood for, especially the "Old Army," but, to use Pickett's metaphor, while the Union was "a neighbor," Virginia was "family" with first claim on their loyalty. Lee expressed similar sentiments when he wrote to his sister on the day he resigned his commission that he could not "raise his hand against his relatives, his children, and his home."[5]

Concerning the greatest sectional issue of the day, slavery, Lee was the more ambiguous of the two. In fact, for a Virginia aristocrat, he was quite enlightened, regarding the institution to be "a moral and political evil in any Country."[6] Pickett accepted the superiority of whites as part of the natural order of things without questioning his assumptions. He did not try to puzzle out the moral right and wrong of it. Both men had personal black servants whom they treated with dignity and fondness.[7]

When the Civil War came, both resigned their commissions to follow their native state into the Confederacy. Lee left the service on April 20, 1861, and promptly accepted command of all Virginia forces. When the seniority list of Army officers was drawn up by the Confederate government, Robert E. Lee ranked third behind Samuel Cooper and Albert S. Johnston. Pickett dragged out the decision much longer than necessary, not resigning his commission until July 1861, while on duty at San Juan Island, Washington Territory. He did not present himself in Richmond until the middle of September, following an arduous and thrilling return from the Pacific Northwest. His first appointment was in the nascent Confederate Regular Army at the rank of major in the artillery, but he soon received a second appointment as a colonel of infantry in the Virginia provisional forces, and this was the springboard to his subsequent promotions.[8]

From this point on their careers followed different arcs, but ultimately both men became what is known in the study of popular culture as "super icons"—personalities who mysteriously transcend their own place in time and history to become legendary figures. Such men, say the experts, have "an incredibly magnetic personality that succeeding generations are drawn to without understanding." In the end the image becomes larger than the man; simply invoking the super icon's name touches a wellspring of emotions among the faithful. Thus heroes become gods and scoffers become heretics.[9]

The process by which men are transformed into super icons is well illustrated by Robert E. Lee and George Pickett. Lee has been variously called "the embodiment of the Lost Cause...the realized King Arthur," and "the flower of chivalry," while about Pickett it has been said, "Every boy growing up in this land...had continually before his eyes the vision, and heard always in his ears the clamorous hoofbeats, of a glorious swashbuckler, compounded of Jeb Stuart, the golden-locked Pickett, and the sudden and terrible Forrest...forever charging the cannon's mouth with the Southern battle flag." Even a Confederate staff officer who did not like Pickett personally admitted that, "Pickett's charge at Gettysburg stirs every heart that beats for great deeds, and will forever live in song and story."[10] An anonymous Pickett admirer proclaimed him the "Bayard of the Confederacy" and also compared him to Napoleon's marshals as *un grand homme de guerre* (a great warrior), thus implicitly casting Lee in the role of Napoleon to Pickett's Marshals Ney or Grouchy. Ironically, another editorialist trumped Pickett's "Bayard of the Confederacy" when he declared Lee to be "the Bayard of America."[11]

Considered as part of the Southern pantheon, they were *dux bellorum* or "war leaders" of the Confederacy. In medieval romantic literature such leaders exhibited great prowess and fierce patriotism, and they accomplished marvelous deeds; in short, they were suitable subjects for legends. And legends aplenty surround both Lee and Pickett.

Every legend has a defining moment. For Lee and Pickett it is Gettysburg. In the minds of most chroniclers of the Civil War, as well as in the public imagination, their fates intersect at the small Pennsylvania town on July 3, 1863 in the grand style of Greek tragedy. The near-mythic connection has only been reaffirmed by the 1975 publication of Michael Shaara's Pulitzer-prize-winning novel, *The Killer Angels* and its subsequent movie version, *Gettysburg* (1993). We remember the battle paradoxically as Lee's most sublime moment and at the same time his greatest failure as a commander—both true statements. It was also Pickett's finest hour as the nominal leader of the climactic third-day assault which bears his name, a charge ordered by Lee against all advice. Yet, while their names can never be separated from the events at Gettysburg, their actual wartime relationship began months before Gettysburg and stretched well beyond Appomattox. It was a relationship which played a crucial role in Confederate fortunes during the last two years of the war forcing Lee to depend on his discredited lieutenant on more than one battlefield.

George Pickett was just one of dozens of general officers who served under Robert E. Lee and were transformed by the association. Lee had deeper relationships with some of the others, based on mutual respect and simpatico. Thomas J. Jackson, James Longstreet, and A. P. Hill, for instance, fall into this category. The taciturn Longstreet had a relationship with Lee that he described as "affectionate, confidential, and even tender, from first to last." Lee displayed a genuine fatherly regard for Pickett's cousin, Brigadier General Henry Heth, for reasons not entirely clear, and he wept when he learned of the death of the gallant Jeb Stuart.[12] In terms of wartime significance, the bond between Jackson and Lee has been rightly called the most successful partnership in U.S. military history despite its lack of intimacy. And recently there has been much attention focused on the "always cordial and warm" personal relationship between Lee and President Jefferson Davis which played such a crucial role in formulating Confederate military policy during four years of war.[13]

Both the Lee-Jackson and Lee-Davis relationships are worthy of study to see why they worked, but in the case of the Lee-Pickett relationship its significance derives from why it did not work. Compared to Lee-Davis or Lee-Jackson, the Lee-Pickett tandem did not formulate war policy or produce a mystical meeting of two like minds. But in the grand scheme of things it proved very nearly as significant albeit for all the wrong reasons.

In his own mind, Pickett always fancied himself a part of the inner circle of officers surrounding the commander of the Army of Northern Virginia, a delusion perpetuated by LaSalle Corbell Pickett in her popular writings after the war. Truth be told, Pickett was, as one scholar has characterized him, "one who sulked upon the outskirts of the Lee cult" because Lee was more cognizant of Pickett's character flaws than even Pickett himself.[14] Pickett could never ingratiate himself into Lee's inner circle, and as the war went on, he was pushed further and further away.

3 Pickett's Niche in the Army of Northern Virginia

Before the Gettysburg campaign, Lee and Pickett had only a nodding professional acquaintance with each other. Colonels (Lee's highest prewar rank) and captains (Pickett's pre-war rank) did not move in the same social circles even if their respective duties had not kept them far apart, which they did. While both called Virginia home, neither one had seen that home very much in the antebellum period. The pre-war U.S. army was small enough that every officer knew practically every other officer, but by reputation, not on a first-name basis. Pickett had never served under the older man before June 1862. From that date until the Gettysburg campaign, their perfunctory relationship was defined by official orders and dry reports which did not include any personal correspondence.

Lee had spent most of the first thirteen months of the war either commanding clerks in Richmond as President Davis' military adviser or on special assignments to South Carolina and western Virginia. During this same period, Colonel Pickett was performing the thankless task of guarding the lower Rappahannock River, a dead-end posting he greatly resented. In February 1862 Pickett received his brigadier general's commission. He was reunited on the Peninsula with his old friend James Longstreet, known as "Old Peter" since his West Point days because of his supposed resemblance to the famous apostle. This was indeed a stroke of luck for Pickett because not only were the two men friends from way back, but Longstreet had a way of bringing out the best in difficult or under-performing subordinates, most notably Richard H. (Dick) Anderson and George Pickett.[1] More than that, Longstreet's opinions were highly esteemed by Robert E. Lee so that a personal recommendation or request by Old Pete was usually all it took to get an endorsement from the "Old Man."

The fighting of May 31-June 1 on the Peninsula finally brought the two men together in the same army: Lee took over the South's principal army (soon to be known as the Army of Northern Virginia) after Joseph Johnston was wounded in the Battle of Seven Pines, and Pickett's Virginia brigade was a part of that same army. In this way, George Pickett became one of the celebrated officers known as "Lee's Lieutenants."

Lee soon set about shaping the army to fit his own personal standards. In the process, some men proved more malleable than others. The dapper brigadier and the stern commanding general were definitely not cut from the same cloth. Pickett was flamboyant, impetuous, and self-indulgent. He frequently experienced bouts of moodiness and resented any attempt to rein in his free spirit. Oftentimes, he let his emotions overrule his better judgment. Lee, on the other hand, was reserved, conscientious, and highly disciplined, although never afraid to show his emotions. This latter trait actually seemed to endear him to his men all the more. One side which he usually kept hidden was the tendency to be "a little sarcastic and savage upon [his] men sometimes."[2] In the handful of recorded instances when this trait manifested itself, however, it was directed against men whom Lee felt had shirked their duty.

Lee had a dark side, too, of which the withering sarcasm noted by Hunton and others, was only one facet. The beloved image of the kindly grandfather figure, always taking failure on his own shoulders while chiding erring subordinates in only the mildest tones, is an incomplete picture. He could work himself up into a "furious passion" on occasion, as Eppa Hunton observed, and when he did get mad on such occasions, "he was mad all over." Charles Marshall, an aide on his staff who knew him better than most, said his "gentle" side was reserved for "domestic and social life, for fondling children or for kind expostulation with erring youth." When provoked by members of his command, his face became flushed and the veins popped out on his temples. He could humiliate an officer as he did the gallant and oft-wounded General Samuel McGowan at the Battle of the Wilderness, by merely asking rhetorically, "My God, General McGowan! Is this splendid brigade of yours running like a flock of geese?"

Library of Congress, Washington, D.C.

"Lee at Chancellorsville, May 2, 1863" (artist unknown). Lee's remarkable rapport with his troops is on display here. No other Confederate officer provoked such adulation among the common soldiers. He was loved and respected by almost all.

As the war dragged on and his physical ailments mounted along with his cares, he became more irascible and hypercritical toward subordinates, and he had never suffered fools gladly under the best of circumstances. The temperamental, the incompetent, the bombastic, all received short shrift from the man who considered duty and honor to be sacred trusts and personal comfort and safety to be iniquitous.[3]

As a commander, Lee could be reckless at times, but it was the calculated risk-taking of the professional gambler, as at Chancellorsville and Antietam. He was willing to place his fate in the hands of subordinates whom he knew and trusted. He also expected his lieutenants to "fight their troops well and take good care of them." More than that, he wanted men of strong moral character around him. For Lee this meant men who were "true, honest and brave; [have] a single eye to the good of the service and spare no exertion to accomplish [their] objective."[4] Fighters and excuse-makers need not apply. Officers who failed to measure up to Lee's standards, such as Benjamin Huger, Theophilus Holmes, W.H.C. Whiting, and John B. Magruder, were quickly shipped out of the Army of Northern Virginia. Lee's high expectations coupled with an unfailing trust in his officers—at least until they proved they were not deserving of that trust—could be extremely intimidating to the very men who worshipped him. Ulysses Grant, who knew both Lee and Pickett very well, once mused, "He [Lee] was a large, austere man, and I judge difficult of approach to his subordinates."[5] Men of abundant self-confidence and demonstrated talents had nothing to fear but woe to officers whose bombast exceeded their talents or who possessed over-inflated egos.

The small matter of hair style typified much about the two men's personalities. Lee wore his prematurely white hair cut to a conventional length. Pickett, on the other hand, was inordinately proud of his long, wispy locks. He wore his hair in perfumed ringlets, a fact which shocked some of his fellow officers when they first met him.[6] Lee's only concession to fashion was a full beard of quite conservative length which he grew during his western Virginia campaign in 1861 and never shaved off afterward. On a deeper level, their characters were also far apart. Pickett was quick to lay the blame for failure on others, a trait which did not endear him to fellow officers who often became the scapegoats in his reports. Lee was just as quick to shoulder the blame for the failures of his subordinates, as well as to admit his own failures. These respective traits stand out clearly in the after-action reports they filed during the war.

As a matter of principle, Lee placed honor and duty above all else. Pickett, by contrast, was a dedicated *bon vivant* who never let duty interfere with having a good time. This attitude made him popular with certain fellow officers like cavalrymen Tom Rosser and Fitzhugh Lee, the commanding general's nephew, who were similarly inclined. It also colored his view of military discipline, which was highly subjective. Pickett was notoriously hard on his men but maintained a different standard for himself. His guiding stars were not honor and duty but pride and self-interest. There was no more unbridgeable gulf between Robert E. Lee and George Pickett than this.

While Lee knew about Pickett, he did not know him personally, and had little reason to take notice of him until the events of June 27, 1862. That was the date of Gaines' Mill, the bloodiest battle in the eastern theater to that point. It cost the Army of Northern Virginia 9,000 men (vs. some 6,000 Federals), but it was an especially notable day for Robert E. Lee because it was his first battlefield victory, marking the beginning of that mystical relationship between the man and the army that would ultimately leave an indelible stamp on American history. One of those 9,000 casualties that day was Brigadier General George Pickett, who won his "red badge of courage" leading his men at Gaines' Mill, and along with it, glowing reviews for his performance.

The army was without Pickett's services for the next three months while he recuperated at home from a severe shoulder wound. During those months, it fought the campaigns of Second Manassas and Antietam, and aggressive commanders like Jeb Stuart and John Bell Hood forged their way to the forefront of the officer ranks, in the process making a lasting impression on the mind of the commanding general. It was a crucial time that saw Lee gauging the strengths and weaknesses of his various lieutenants by observing them in the fire of battle. Those who won his trust and respect became Lee's "military family," and there was, as his adjutant Walter Taylor pointed out, "a degree of camaraderie [among them] that was perfectly delightful."[7] Meanwhile, George Pickett, apart from his one heroic performance, remained something of a cipher to his commanding general.

The first official notice that Lee took of Pickett occurred in the fall of 1862 when the Army of Northern Virginia was undergoing its second major reorganization.[8] After the long summer of campaigning in northern Virginia and the aborted invasion of Maryland that ended at Antietam, Lee's army was short of healthy general officers. He set about remedying that deficiency working in conjunction with President Davis and the Confederate Congress. On October 11, the Confederate Senate confirmed Longstreet and Jackson as lieutenant generals, in that order of seniority.[9] As a result of their elevation and recent battlefield losses, there was also an immediate need for four new major generals. Pickett who at the time was Longstreet's senior brigadier, was put forward for one of those openings by his old friend Longstreet. The latter's intention was that Pickett should take over the "larger part" of his old division in the redistribution of troops that was planned.[10] The other major general nominees, pushed by various mentors at this time, were John Bell Hood (by Longstreet), Isaac Trimble (by Jackson), and Jubal Early (Jackson and Lee). All except Pickett had rendered "distinguished service" at Second Manassas, Antietam, or both. More importantly, they had shown themselves capable of handling a division under battlefield conditions. Only Pickett's recommendation was based on past glories.

On October 27 Lee put Pickett's name on the list of officers he desired for division command, submitting it to President Davis for formal nomination.[11] After the usual political log rolling, Hood and Pickett were nominated by the president and confirmed by the Senate. Lee's endorsement alone, however perfunctory, should have been sufficient to assure Pickett's promotion. As Jefferson Davis told a newspaperman some years later, "In General Lee's army...no promotions were made without his special recommendation, and no subordinate retained in his army whom he reported to be incompetent."[12] Undoubtedly, Pickett's Virginia roots, West Point background, and congenial nature also played a part. Lee's lack of personal knowledge of Pickett at this stage actually worked in the latter's favor. The commanding general's choices for division command were somewhat limited using as the principal criteria experience, proven aggressiveness, and West Point training. Unlike his strongly stated opinions of Longstreet, Jackson, and A. P. Hill when the lieutenant general vacancies were filled, Lee did not express his personal opinion on any of the major general candidates in his recommendations to Richmond. The promotions were announced in orders issued from the War Department on November 6.[13]

In making his formal nominations Lee followed a practice which he would follow in future rounds of promotions; he recommended other officers with great potential for future consideration. These were officers who in Lee's mind did not quite make the cut this time, but with a little more seasoning, would be ready to take on greater responsibilities in the near future. Lee singled out Ambrose Powell Hill as an officer deserving of lieutenant generalship in the next round of promotions. Although Pickett was the senior brigade commander of the First Corps, Lee did not cite him for future promotion, reflecting if not reservations, at least a distinct unfamiliarity with the young brigadier.

When Lee reorganized his army a second time in May 1863 following the Battle of Chancellorsville and the death of the beloved Stonewall Jackson, he identified two of his battle-tested major generals as ready for the next step up to lieutenant general's rank—Richard Ewell and Ambrose Powell Hill. Their major generals' commissions antedated that of George Pickett, and both had performed admirably since the Army of Northern Virginia's first campaign under Lee the previous spring. Hill had been on an upward career arc since being promoted to brigadier general in February 1862. Indeed, he was one of the shining lights of the Army of Northern Virginia, and his promotion to corps command came as no surprise. Nor did Ewell's being singled out violate any conventions of the promotion system. The eccentric Virginian had done his apprenticeship under Jackson, and paid for that schooling with the loss of his left leg at the Battle of Groveton. Both Hill and Ewell were aggressive fighters and strict disciplinarians who showed great attention to detail and possessed excellent military instincts. More than that, they were known commodities to Lee. When the commanding general recommended them to fill the two lieutenant generals' openings, he reviewed their qualifications on the basis of close personal observation: "[Ewell] is an honest, brave soldier, who has always done his duty well.... [Hill] I think upon the whole, is the best soldier of his grade with me." Jefferson Davis and the Confederate Congress, as usual, accepted Lee's recommendations without question, and Ewell took over Jackson's old Second Corps while Hill assumed command of the new Third Corps.[14]

As he had done before, Lee prepared the way for future promotions on this occasion by citing at this time both Dick Anderson and John Bell Hood as "capital officers" who would make "good corps commanders" if and when additional openings occurred.[15] George Pickett did not make the cut as lieutenant general material, and no one was pushing him for such a promotion, nor was he on Lee's short list for future consideration. The reasons are not hard to understand when we hold him up beside either Hill or Ewell at this point in the war. Compared to those two worthies, Pickett to date had not "always done his duty well," had let details of drill and camp slide, and had demonstrated a troubling lack of self-discipline. Lee had only to ask such men as Moxley Sorrel, James Longstreet, or Theophilus Holmes to get a fair appraisal of Pickett's on-the-job performance.

On the other side of the ledger, Pickett had shown himself to be a fighter thus far and a popular fellow with his men, and these were both strong factors in his favor. If he was also a romantic, given to impetuous behavior at times and unimpressed with rules and regulations, those were not destructive qualities in and of themselves. The same descriptions could be applied to such well-regarded fighters as Jeb Stuart and Powell Hill. The proof was whether an officer could bring his troops to battle when and where they were needed and, having done that, fight them properly.

The final verdict was not in on Pickett as a major general at the time of Lee's second reorganization. Only in retrospect can we see that his career ran into a brick wall after November 1862, and the name of that brick wall was Robert E. Lee. The irony is that the same man who opened the door for him that fall also slammed that door shut in his face later on. Not only was Pickett not promoted again, but he was not even considered by Lee for further promotion. He was still regarded as a useful member of the Army of Northern Virginia in the months following, but he would never win the full confidence of the man who commanded that army.

Lee's low evaluation of Pickett was not based on mere personal dislike, nor was it peculiar to Lee within the Confederate command structure. Throughout the war Pickett's commanding officers showed time and again that they were not overly impressed by his capabilities. Beginning with Theophilus Holmes when Pickett was a colonel on the Rappahannock in 1861, and going through Longstreet, Beauregard at Petersburg, and ultimately Lee, his superiors occasionally commended his actions, but never pushed him for promotion nor fought to keep him attached to their commands.[16] On this one occasion in the fall of 1862, Pickett slipped through the cracks in the promotional system. Pickett's promotion to major general put him closer to Lee in the army's official hierarchy, but had no immediate effect on their personal relationship.

Library of Congress

A proud George Pickett, in his new major general's uniform, probably taken in Richmond in the fall of 1862.

The Lee-Pickett personal relationship got off to a pleasant enough start with Lee's endorsement of his promotion to major general, but their first clash was not long in coming. It took the form of a formal complaint about the condition of Pickett's new division. During the long winter of inactivity following the Battle of Fredericksburg (December 13, 1862), Lee ordered inspections of all divisions as part of his efforts to keep the army in fighting shape. The inspection report that came back on Pickett's Division, the first since he became a major general, did not please the commanding general, and on January 19, 1863, he wrote to Pickett's corps commander (Longstreet) expressing his deep dissatisfaction with the poor condition of the men. In one brigade, Lee chided, "the articles of war were seldom read, accommodation of the sick bad, and religious exercises neglected." Such seemingly minor matters were detrimental to good military efficiency in Lee's opinion, and he concluded that Pickett and his officers were "not sufficiently attentive to the men [and] not informed as to their condition." The bottom line was, he wanted changes made, not for petty, bureaucratic reasons, but to improve the fighting efficiency of the army. Lee warned Longstreet that, "unless the division and brigade commanders are careful and energetic, nothing can be accomplished."[17]

There is no extant correspondence between Longstreet and Pickett to indicate that the First Corps commander passed on Lee's concerns. However, there is every reason to think that he did, although Longstreet could well have softened the words in consideration of Pickett's sensitive feelings. The important thing is that Lee knew who George Pickett was at this point and did not like what he saw in his new major general. Others also noted around this time that Pickett preferred to leave "the division details to his staff." William Dabney Stuart, a Virginia Military Institute graduate and colonel of the 56th Virginia, suggested that it was the general's romantic obsession that got in the way of his official duties. Slackness at the top of the division was reflected all the way down through the ranks, and Lee did not have the same confidence in Pickett's men that he did other troops in the army.[18]

A couple of months later Lee found what appeared to be the perfect place for Pickett and his slackers. The Confederates received word that the Army of the Potomac's Ninth Corps, soon to have Ambrose Burnside at its head, was being shifted down the Potomac River toward some unknown objective on the Southern coast, most likely southeast Virginia or North Carolina. Alarm bells went off in Richmond as fears of another amphibious mounted attack on the capital were contemplated. Union bases at Suffolk, Virginia, and at New Berne and Washington, North Carolina, were all within striking distance. Lee was pressured by the government to send front-line troops to deal with the situation, though he himself believed that state militia and local garrison detachments could adequately handle it.

Lee's response is interesting. The threat was mostly in Richmond's mind. "The enemy's positions in North Carolina [and southeast Virginia] have always appeared to me to be taken for defense," he wrote Longstreet some time later. Therefore he saw the whole thing as largely much ado about nothing.[19] Yet as a rear area, the south side of the James River was eminently suitable posting for suspect commanders and unreliable troops. Only a month earlier Lee had expressed to Longstreet his displeasure with General Pickett and his band of merry Virginians. Here was the chance to perform a little addition by subtraction, ridding his army of some troublesome elements while taking positive steps to allay the government's fears.

On or about Valentine's Day, 1863, Lee detached Pickett's Division and put them on the road to Richmond to shield the capital and watch the coastal beachheads of the Federals. He had already offered to send down Major General D. H. Hill to North Carolina "if any benefit will be derived by sending an officer to inspirit or encourage the people." Harvey Hill had distinguished himself to this point mainly by his endless carping and obstreperousness, which had sorely tried Lee's patience. One cannot escape the implication that Lee was cleaning house in his own quiet way. The two major generals had worn out their welcome in the Army of Northern Virginia and the solution of Pickett to Richmond and Hill to North Carolina was a win-win situation for the commanding general.[20]

The shrewd strategem of addition by subtraction however soon came unhinged. A couple of days after sending off Pickett, Lee was forced to ship Hood's Division south, too, with potentially a much bigger impact on the army's fighting strength. Lee did not want to lose Hood's hard-charging soldiers nor their intrepid commander, so this was a much more painful loss to the army in Lee's estimation. The pain was hardly lessened by the need to send Longstreet along with Hood's Division to take charge of the growing operation. This was the result of Longstreet's pestering for independent command and the public's growing alarm about the seriousness of the threat from southeast Virginia.[21]

At the time Lee dispatched Pickett, the whole affair was small potatoes, and Lee's chief concern had been keeping his irrepressible major general on a tight leash. He was not eager to launch any new operations on a heretofore quiet front, and, remembering well Pickett's hot-headedness on other fields, was determined not to allow him too much latitude in his new command. The last thing Lee desired was to stir up a hornet's nest with an aggressive campaign that would bring the enemy swarming out of his enclaves. Such a campaign would wind up draining additional troops from more important operations in northern Virginia. Pickett's job was to be prudently watchful and to reassure all the Nervous Nellies that things were well in hand. Lee instructed his major general to take up a position south of the James and "await further orders," keeping himself ready to defend Petersburg "if necessary."[22]

Despite being in a rear area, Richmond might have been a high-profile posting, but Pickett was not posted to the Confederate capital *per se*. His orders from Lee were, first, to "halt on the Chickahominy" north of Richmond, then subsequently to "take position below Richmond on the right or left bank of the [James] river." In this way he was kept from assuming even nominal command of the Department of Richmond, which remained firmly in General G. W. Smith's hands at this point. He had to content himself with marching his infantry through the city on February 21, to the "cheers and hurried greetings" of the populace, on their way south.[23] Pickett's precautionary orders to do nothing more than wait and watch took away what little latitude of action he might otherwise have exercised in this latest assignment. He was to be squarely under somebody's thumb at all times. Lee told the Secretary of War in no uncertain terms on February 16, "I must request you to give him orders," and a few days later, with Longstreet on the way, Lee made sure his loose cannon was once more under the First Corps commander's oversight. Pickett was directed, through the Adjutant General's office, to "report without delay to Lieutenant General J. Longstreet, commanding Department of Virginia and North Carolina."[24]

Pickett, for all practical purposes, had been passed from Lee to Seddon to Longstreet without being given so much as an inch of maneuvering room. At the same time, he was effectively denied the pleasures of Richmond society which he had so enjoyed earlier. Taken altogether, Pickett's first detached assignment from the Army of Northern Virginia could hardly be construed as a vote of confidence.

By comparison, when D. H. Hill and G. W. Smith were detached earlier from the Army of Northern Virginia and sent on the same errand, their orders had allowed them the flexibility to respond to situations as they saw fit; they acted as independent commanders. Pickett essentially was left in limbo with little power to command, and no idea what was expected of him, even when he commanded the only true fighting force in the department. It was an awkward and demeaning position which could be interpreted, as one scholar has done, as punishment for the recent negative inspection report. "The seeds of discord" between Robert E. Lee and George E. Pickett may well have been first planted here."[25]

Lee's thinking in all this is not hard to discern. As a rule he did not like to disperse his army to guard threatened points far away from the main arena of action in northern Virginia. He only did so to placate Richmond. Left to his own devices, he much preferred to keep his forces together awaiting an opportunity to strike a decisive blow at the enemy's army. He put little stock in unconfirmed reports that the Union Ninth Corps (or perhaps the Second Corps, according to different sources) were descending on Suffolk, Virginia, but if true, he assured the War Department disingenuously, "General Pickett's division will be ample to resist it."[26]

At this point, Lee was more concerned with the threat posed by General Hooker and the Army of the Potomac in northern Virginia. The only division he was willing, perhaps even eager, to give up to chase phantoms in southeastern Virginia, was George Pickett's. Sending Pickett carried the added attraction of being a "safe" arrangement as conceived, because just as soon as Pickett was beyond Lee's reach, he would come under the watchful eye of either Gustavus Smith (Department of Richmond), James A. Seddon (War Department), or Samuel French (department commander for southern Virginia after January 27).

Additional demands coming from the Secretary of War for Longstreet and Hood threw Lee's plans awry. Compared to Lee's gratuitous offer of Pickett's Division, it took some real arm-twisting by James Seddon to pry both the First Corps commander and Hood's Division away from the Army of Northern Virginia. Their departure left Lee with only 62,000 troops on the Rappahannock line facing the man known as "Fighting Joe" Hooker with more than twice that number. Only the War Department's insistence persuaded him to part with them.[27]

Longstreet's subsequent assumption of department command on February 25, and his organization of the glory-seeking Suffolk campaign should not obscure the fact that this whole thing began as a temporary exile of George Pickett to the war's backwater. Any hopes Pickett might have had for independent command died when Longstreet arrived on the scene. In taking over the Department of Virginia and North Carolina, Longstreet received the sweeping authority Pickett had been denied. No James Seddon or Gustavus Smith or anyone else looked over his shoulder. Old Pete exercised command over all Confederate garrison troops between Richmond and Wilmington, plus his own two divisions (Hood and Pickett). Pickett dutifully reported to Longstreet and was posted in Petersburg, midway between the capital and Longstreet's operations on the Blackwater River.

With discretion to conduct his own operations, Longstreet wasted no time launching an offensive campaign and foraging expedition in the eastern sector of his department. Pickett found his division being stripped away, a brigade at a time, to reinforce other commands, while Pickett himself cooled his heels at Petersburg. Eventually, he and his three remaining brigades found themselves building earthworks south of Suffolk. Frustrated by what he considered a lack of meaningful assignment, the major general spent his time asking Longstreet for leave and riding off to court LaSalle Corbell in nearby Nansemond County, Virginia.[28]

Pickett and his division remained separated from Lee and the Army of Northern Virginia through the spring of 1863, and came close to being sent even farther afield, to the western theater. Joe Johnston, commanding Confederate forces in Mississippi, was calling desperately for reinforcements at this time, and Richmond favored sending Pickett to the rescue. Jefferson Davis and his Secretary of War James Seddon were the two principal advocates of this idea. Lee opposed the transfer on the sensible grounds that Longstreet needed Pickett's Division to complete foraging operations in southeast Virginia. The so-called Suffolk campaign was crucial to re-supplying the Army of Northern Virginia for the upcoming campaign season. And once those operations were over, Lee proposed bringing Longstreet, with Pickett's and Hood's Divisions, back to the Army of Northern Virginia. Pickett's Division and its commander were simply pawns in the highly dubious strategy of shifting troops back and forth between the eastern and western theaters to meet the latest crisis.[29]

Even after the Suffolk campaign concluded in May, Pickett was not promptly recalled to the army as were Longstreet and Hood. When those two were ordered to rejoin Lee on the Rappahannock, Pickett was left behind. Instead, he received special orders from Secretary of War James Seddon to "proceed as rapidly as possible...to the city of Richmond, where further instructions will meet [you]."[30]

What Seddon had in mind was to ship Pickett with his division out west to reinforce John Pemberton who was then facing Grant at Vicksburg. Again, Lee went to bat for retaining Pickett with the Army of Northern Virginia. Not only, Lee argued, was he facing the latest annual Union offensive against Richmond, but he was working on his own plans to carry the war into the North. He felt Pickett's Division could be better employed with the Army of Northern Virginia than on some wild-goose chase out west, but graciously conceded, "If necessary, order Pickett at once." It was not so much Pickett himself whom Lee feared losing as his 5,000 proven veterans, and he carefully expressed himself in these terms in an exchange of telegrams with Seddon. The Army of Northern Virginia simply could not afford to lose Pickett's Division if it was to be expected to conduct offensive operations. "Its removal from this army will be sensibly felt," he warned in characteristic Lee understatement. By implication, George Pickett might be expendable to the Army of Northern Virginia but not his division. This is a telling distinction by a commanding general who was never shy about informing Richmond precisely what he needed although always in deferential and temperate tones. In the end Lee won his battle to keep Pickett with the Army of Northern Virginia. On May 16 J.B. Jones, a clerk in the War Department, noted in his diary, "It appears, after the consultation of the generals and the President yesterday, it was resolved not to send Pickett's division to Mississippi."[31]

So Pickett did not go west, but neither did he march with Lee's army when it headed north in June 1863. Instead, he found himself shifted all around Richmond like a knight on a chess board, first to Hanover Junction twenty miles north of the city, then to Falling Creek, eight miles south of the city.[32] He refused to behave as a proper "knight" however, much preferring to take advantage of his situation by trying to arrange meetings with LaSalle Corbell in Richmond. He soon found that his men—native Virginians all—were just as eager to get out of camp and take in the sights of the city before they were sent off to another distant battlefield. Many of them had close friends and relatives in the Confederate capital. Pickett could hardly deny them the same privileges he himself was taking, with the result that both the major general and a number of his officers got to see a lot of scenery from train windows going back and forth to Richmond. This lax attitude about duty in Pickett's Division, starting at the top, was brought once more to Lee's attention, although at the time the commanding general was busy planning his offensive into Pennsylvania. From Lee's headquarters came orders prohibiting the soldiers of Pickett's Division from leaving camp and riding the trains into Richmond, and that restriction was even extended to the division commander himself, a pointed slap on the wrist.[33] Pickett's romantic escapades were becoming the talk of the army, and the commanding general evidently was not pleased with such behavior, or what Moxley Sorrel called "carpet-knight doings."[34]

For his part, Pickett complained petulantly about having his wings clipped. He wrote to Major General Arnold Elzey, a fellow West Point graduate and casualty of Gaines' Mill who at this time was commanding the Department of Richmond, saying, "this circumstance" was a "great detriment to the facilities of expediting military movements of importance." Pickett's convoluted syntax was only exceeded by his convoluted reasoning, neither of which impressed Lee. On three different occasions during the space of two weeks Pickett sought to overturn Lee's travel restrictions, protesting directly in writing to the commanding general. He received no reply— "not even the scratch of a pen," as he put it in his letter to Elzey. He asked Elzey to carry his complaint straight to the Secretary of War, thus attempting to go over Lee's head, but this approach got no reply either from Elzey or James Seddon.[35]

Lee did not respond directly to Pickett's complaints, but only ordered him "to be ready to move at a moment's notice with three days' rations." The orders included no destination or route, and no hint of the commanding general's plans for his major general.[36] Pickett chafed at being kept in the dark, but could do nothing except await Lee's further instructions. It seemed as if he were going to miss the Gettysburg campaign the same way he had missed the Antietam campaign—by being left behind.

Pickett continued to exasperate Lee, and vice versa. The army commander issued orders for Pickett to send some wagons to a place called Newton in order to collect supplies before proceeding on to Tappahannock. Finding no such place on any of his maps, Pickett telegraphed Lee twice for further instructions, and twice he received no answer. He fumed to the only person apparently willing to listen to him, General Elzey: "As usual from those headquarters, [I] receive no reply."[37]

Lee had not forgotten about George Pickett, however. After Pickett's testy communique about his latest assignment, Lee wrote to apologize that "my dispatch of yesterday might not have been sufficiently plain." Then Lee patiently explained the obvious, viz., "that my object in moving your command toward Tappahannock was to meet the enemy." From Tappahannock, Pickett's Division would be able to secure the army's right flank against a thrust up the York or Rappahannock rivers, and in particular guard the important railroad junction at Hanover.[38]

Lee's dispositions were, in fact, well conceived because a "marauding expedition" of Yankees was headed Pickett's way. Lee, as he was wont to do with his commanders on the scene, allowed Pickett considerable latitude to implement his orders, telling him, "If you learn that the enemy has retired and is beyond your grasp, I desire you to return to your position. If they come within your reach, and you can do so with advantage, strike at them."[39]

Still, Lee was not entirely comfortable with the idea of giving Pickett free rein. He also took the highly unusual step of sending a duplicate copy of Pickett's orders to Johnston Pettigrew, who had recently brought his brigade of North Carolinians up from New Berne. Pettigrew must have scratched his head at Lee's instructions to pass them along to Pickett and inform headquarters when he had done so. This put Pettigrew in the awkward position of bird-dogging Pickett which, as it turned out, was a good idea.

Still miffed at being left out of the Big Show, Pickett showed little enthusiasm for chasing down Yankee raiders who numbered no more than 400 in his vicinity. He moved barely five miles from his base at Hanover Junction before turning back. Meanwhile, the Yankees plundered and burned Prince William County at will before fleeing in boats back down the Mattapony River whence they had come. Lee, unaware that the enemy had accomplished their purpose and departed, told A. P. Hill in apparent frustration, "I fear Pickett did not go far enough...I have telegraphed him that he must drive them back."[40]

But George Pickett had his own agenda, which did not include chasing around the countryside after phantom Yankees, and he made no secret of it. On June 6, Pettigrew reported to General Elzey in Richmond that the love-struck major general was on his way to the capital again."[41] Pickett's latest courting mission was cut short however, when Lee ordered him north to Culpeper Court House with the intention of reuniting his division with the rest of the army.[42]

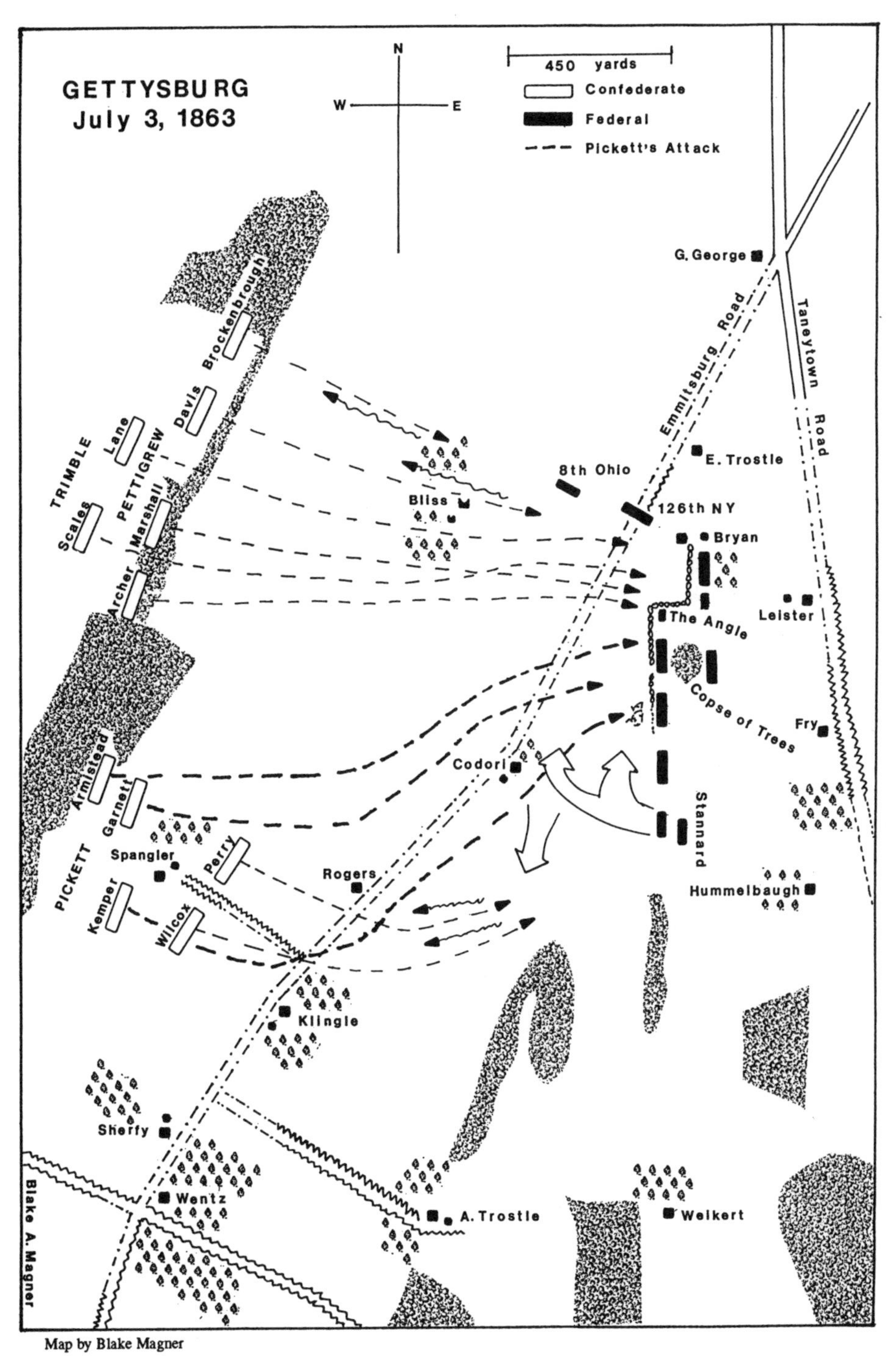

Map by Blake Magner

Pickett's Charge

4 Gettysburg: Shining, Bitter Moment for Lee and Pickett

George Pickett hurried north with mixed feelings. On the one hand he was glad to be going back to the main show where he could show Lee what he and his division could do. On the other hand, he was sorrowful at being called away from his beloved whom he was already planning to marry as soon as possible. On the way north he was once again rudely reminded of what a small cog he was in Confederate military operations. His division, rather than being hurled at the Yankees as a mighty fighting machine, was broken up even while marching toward a date with glory. Passing through the vital rail center of Hanover Junction, Montgomery Corse's Brigade peeled off and remained behind. This was the second brigade Pickett had lost in a matter of weeks. Earlier, when he came up from southeast Virginia, he had left Micah Jenkins' Brigade in front of Suffolk. With his division now reduced by two-fifths, Pickett was inclined to blame Lee for decisions which had actually been made in Richmond. He protested directly to Lee's headquarters emphasizing that it was "in no spirit of complaint" that he asked for at least one of his brigades back. This was not for himself alone, he told Lee, "but merely as an act of justice to my division and myself, for it is well known that a small division will be expected to do the same amount of hard service as a large one, and as the army is now divided, my division will be, I think, decidedly the weakest." Hoping to get what he wanted with sugar rather than his usual vitriol, he signed off with words reminiscent of a medieval humility formula: "Hoping the general commanding will give this request his consideration..."[1]

Despite the sweet words and urgent plea, his protest did not bring him any additional brigades. But it did provoke a sharp reply from Walter Taylor, Lee's adjutant-general and the man who usually served as the commanding general's lightning rod. "There is no other brigade in the army which could be assigned to [your] division at this time," he informed Pickett with finality.[2]

What Pickett could not understand was that the commanding general wanted the brigades just as badly as his division commander and was arguing strenuously with both Richmond and D. H. Hill, department commander in North Carolina, trying to get them. Three weeks into the campaign and already deep in enemy country, Lee was still petitioning Richmond to return the absent brigades, saying, "[I] wish Corse's brigade to be ordered to rejoin its division under Pickett as soon as possible." What he got instead was a lengthy letter from President Davis explaining the military necessity behind keeping them right where they were, and even that was not delivered, being intercepted by Union cavalry on June 2.[3] Both Lee and Pickett were frustrated by the situation, but the former accepted it as something beyond his control while the latter stubbornly believed that Lee was still pursuing a personal vendetta against him. That belief was apparent in the tone of his communiques with Lee's headquarters.

On top of everything else, Pickett felt so unhappy to be marching away from LaSalle that he was counting the days until he could get back to her. Thoughts of battle and conquest were the last things on his mind despite the fact that he was with an army of invasion pushing deep into enemy country. He wrote LaSalle that he took no joy in being a "Conquering Hero."[4] He also took little interest in most of the routine duties of command, although he could still be a brutal taskmaster when so inclined. On June 24 he ordered the men assembled to witness the execution of a deserter from the 18th Virginia Infantry, a spectacle intended to serve as "an example and a deterrent" to any others who might also be feeling homesick.[5]

Three days earlier Lee had addressed a different sort of discipline problem when he issued his famous General Order No. 72 governing the conduct of the army while it was on Northern soil:

The commanding general considers that no greater disgrace could befall the army than the perpetration of the barbarous outrages upon the innocent and defenseless and wanton destruction of private property that have marked the course of the enemy in our own country. Such proceedings not only disgrace the perpetrators and all connected with them, but are subversive of the discipline and efficiency of the army and destructive of the ends of our present movements. It must be remembered that we make war only on armed men, and that we cannot take vengeance for the wrongs our people have suffered without lowering ourselves in the eyes of all whose abhorrence has been excited by the atrocities of our enemy and offending against Him to whom vengeance belongeth, without whose favor and support our efforts must prove in vain.[6]

It is no surprise to find the twin themes of efficiency and discipline mixed in with a message of spiritual purity. The appeal to his men to march onward as "Christian Soldiers" was vintage Lee, and one of the principal reasons why they loved him so dearly. It was more than sanctimonious claptrap. Even the most unchristian among them also understood, as one Texas colonel explained, that "when Massa Robert issued an order it meant, 'You must and shall obey.'"[7] Still, even such a noble appeal as this fell on deaf ears in some quarters. The Pennsylvania countryside was rich and heretofore untouched by war. To hungry and ill-clad Southern boys, that was an open invitation to pillage and plunder, and there was more than a touch of payback in their actions. Many of Pickett's Virginians had witnessed the destructive effects of war on their own families and homesteads. They looked forward to exacting just retribution until Lee's orders came down.

Some officers proved more diligent than others in riding herd on their men, a discrepancy that was soon common knowledge throughout the army. General Garnett was one who agreed with Lee's very proper desire to "preserve the discipline in our army...which would inevitably be destroyed were indiscriminate plundering allowed," but he also admitted that the orders would be "generally disapproved" within his own brigade. Lee's desires and orders notwithstanding, no public punishments were meted out to violators. When several members of Pickett's Division disregarded Order No. 72, and it was subsequently reported to him, he responded breezily, "We are not obliged to do everything General Lee says." His men proceeded on their rowdy way, relieved even of the pretense of obeying the commanding general's orders. Pickett had already shown on more than one occasion that he considered himself above the normal rules and regulations. He was a firm believer in the age-old military dictum that "rank has its privileges," and he never let pass any opportunity to stretch the rules to suit his own whims.[8]

When Pickett finally caught up with Lee and the rest of the army as they made their way through Maryland, his first personal contact with the commander was hardly pleasant for a man of Pickett's proud and sensitive temperament. At Hagerstown on or about June 26, a young lady with stars in her eyes approached a group of Confederate officers which included Lee and Pickett to ask for a lock of the famous General Lee's hair. Lee replied mischievously that he had no lock of hair to spare for a keepsake, but "he was confident that General Pickett would be pleased to give [up] one of his curls." Lee liked a good joke, and his staff members were well acquainted with his teasing, often sardonic sense of humor. While everyone else within earshot enjoyed a hearty laugh, Pickett was not so amused. It did not help that he was already in a foul mood because just the day before his division had been forced to stand aside while brigades of A. P. Hill's Corps were allowed to pass ahead of them on the road. Besides the delay while they waited, this meant that Pickett's men had to eat the Third Corps' dust, plus there was the added insult that the farther back a unit was assigned in the order of march, the less prestige it could claim.[9]

This otherwise insignificant encounter is noteworthy as the first reported evidence that Lee even knew who George Pickett was outside of their official correspondence. It also shows a biting sense of humor on Lee's part which the Confederate commander usually kept well hidden. Only a few intimates knew that behind the austere facade, he possessed a genuine "exuberance of spirit."[10] By contrast, Pickett took himself very seriously, and found jokes at his expense decidedly unfunny.

Being slighted by his commanding officer soon took a more serious form than mere jokes about hair. On June 30 Longstreet received orders to advance with most of his corps on Cashtown. Pickett and his division, however, were left behind at Chambersburg specifically "by General Lee's orders."[11] Pickett was "to guard the trains and secure the rear" until such time as he could be relieved by General John Imboden's cavalry division.

His men made themselves at home. They had already spent three days at that place engaging in an orgy of destruction directed against the extensive local railroad facilities. But now instead of being called up to fight they were being left behind to pick cherries while the rest of the corps moved on closer to a battle everyone knew was coming.[12]

It was not until July 1 at 5:30 p.m., after the battle had already been joined, that Pickett was ordered up, and then his orders came from Longstreet's headquarters, not Lee's. One must be careful not to read too much into this, but guarding trains and securing rear areas are not the tasks ordinarily given to a valuable fighting unit. A commanding general ordinarily places his best fighting units at the front, not the rear of his army when he is about to give battle.[13]

Up at 2:00 a.m. on July 2, Pickett hustled his men down the road the twenty-six miles from Chambersburg to Gettysburg, sending his adjutant general Walter Harrison ahead to report to Lee at his headquarters as soon as they arrived on the field in the late afternoon. Pickett believed that with a brief rest they could go straight into battle, but Lee thought otherwise. The commanding general virtually ignored Pickett, instructing Harrison to, "Tell General Pickett I shall not want him [or his troops] this evening...and I will send him word when I want them." The division bivouacked on the Cashtown Road while their commander impatiently marked time as a spectator to the late afternoon fighting. That night, when Lee began planning his July 3 moves, those plans centered on using Pickett's Division in an early morning attack, but no orders were sent to the commander of the division to bring up his troops by dawn. With only a vague idea of what he was to do, Pickett did not get his men up to the front until hours after daylight.[14]

The Battle of Gettysburg should have been George Pickett's shining moment of glory, his chance to prove that the confidence placed in him when he was promoted to division commander was deserved. It was Pickett's first opportunity under Lee to demonstrate the qualities that a major general should possess. If he were going to redeem himself for his demonstrated inadequacies in matters of drill and discipline, it would be as a combat officer in the cauldron of battle. That was, after all, why he had been promoted in the first place, as a reward for his performance in the spring of 1862 during the battles in front of Richmond.

Yet ironically, and for a variety of reasons, Pickett played a remarkably insignificant role in the three-day battle that is so closely linked with his name. From the beginning of the campaign he had seemed to be the odd man out. His virtual snubbing on the third day was part of a pattern established at the beginning of the campaign. George Pickett was not a commander whose opinions were sought out or whose judgment in military matters was trusted by his superiors, or even sometimes by his own staff. When on the morning of July 3, Armistead's Brigade had a hard time finding a place to squeeze into the battle line, Major Harrison went looking for General Longstreet to resolve the dilemma, only to be told curtly by Longstreet that it was Pickett's problem and he should solve it.[15]

As originally conceived and then modified by Lee, the battle plan for July 3 did not need any input from George Pickett. It was conceived in Lee's mind and reluctantly modified after conversation with Longstreet in the early morning hours, and although Pickett's Division was to play a central role in the plan, the major general himself was left out when all the important decisions were being made. At the conclusion of his early morning conference with Longstreet at the latter's headquarters, Lee ordered his First Corps commander to "prepare Pickett's Division for the attack."[16] More than twelve hours had elapsed from the time Pickett first reported to Lee, to when he was informed of his role in the day's battle plan. For Pickett it was a time of wondering and waiting.

After designating the objective and deciding on the troops to be used, Lee left the details of the attack up to Longstreet. The First Corps commander moved troops and guns around, conferred with his junior officers, and occasionally gazed apprehensively toward Cemetery Ridge. He was later accused of dragging his heels in making the necessary preparations, but he himself said that "most of the morning was consumed" waiting for Pickett's men to come up and get into position.[17]

Pickett himself felt no particular sense of urgency. He spent a leisurely morning getting his troops into position before joining Longstreet under an apple tree on the Spangler farm in the forenoon. They were there when General Lee rode up to discuss the day's plans further with Longstreet. Longstreet was still decidedly unenthused about Lee's plan, adamantly maintaining that no troops on earth could dislodge the enemy from his position on Cemetery Ridge. Pickett, listening closely, chimed in that he thought his division could "drive them from his front," which were just the words Lee wanted to hear. The men in the ranks nearby seemed to agree with Pickett's optimism more than Longstreet's gloomy prognosis.[18]

Among the officers who provided input to Lee's thinking that morning, besides Longstreet, were A.P. Hill, Henry Heth, and members of Lee's staff including Walter Taylor, Charles Venable and A.L. Long. Yet the impression remains that of all the staff and field officers whose opinions were sought out by Lee, Pickett was an afterthought.

Later that morning Pickett finally joined Lee and other senior officers as they rode about the field discussing troop dispositions and observing the Union position. At 9:00 a.m. Sergeant Levin C. Gayle of the 9th Virginia saw Pickett, Lee, and A.P. Hill "passing up and down our lines" after the men of the division had received their orders. At another point in the morning's preparations Pickett joined Lee and Longstreet in a mounted conference at a time when they were in deep conversation.[19] Pickett's inclusion in these high-level meetings was more a formality in recognition of the crucial role his troops would play in the upcoming assault than because his input was needed. It was Lee's plan and Longstreet's assault. George Pickett needed to be *informed* of Lee's and Longstreet's intentions but not *consulted.* He was the dutiful subordinate allowed to listen in on the war council of his chiefs.

There is another likely reason besides professional courtesy that Pickett was included in those councils, which is found in the words of Longstreet's adjutant, Moxley Sorrel: to make sure he got the plan right. As the staff officer in charge of delivering Longstreet's orders, Sorrel had been told on more than one occasion by his commanding officer to "give [Pickett] things very fully" and even stay with him if necessary in order "to make sure he did not get astray."[20] Whether Pickett was flattered or even fully realized what he was being called upon to do is impossible to say.

In any event, the decision to use Pickett's Division as the centerpiece of the day's action was not a result of Lee's faith in his flamboyant major general but the only reasonable choice available to a commander who desperately needed fresh troops for a major assault into the heart of the enemy's lines. Later, the myth of "Pickett's Election" to occupy the place of honor grew up and was accepted by the survivors themselves as an article of faith to explain their sacrifice that day. As James H. Walker of the 9th Virginia explained: "The impression seemed to be that General Lee had selected the division for this special duty, believing that they could carry Cemetery Heights [Ridge] by assault, and they, having sublime faith in his opinion, started in the charge, satisfied that they would accomplish what he ordered."[21]

The truth is, Pickett's Division was the only unbloodied division in the Army of Northern Virginia on the morning of July 3, 1863. The particular officer at the head of that division was practically irrelevant to Lee's thinking. The commanding general would have made the same decision regardless of who was at the head of "Pickett's Division." Pickett's personal role in the day's action did not become a significant factor until hours later when the assault force was advancing through shell and musket fire on Cemetery Ridge. Since in Lee's thinking the entire assault was carried out "under Longstreet's direction," any role played by George Pickett that day was secondary at best.[22] What was important were Pickett's 5,000 or so determined Virginians.

Beginning on opposite ends of the emotional spectrum, the moods of Lee and Pickett drew closer as the day progressed. While preparing and conferring with his officers in the morning, Lee did not display his usual "quiet, self-possessed confidence;" instead he appeared to be more "careworn..., anxious..., impatient..., nervous...," even "disturbed" than anyone had ever seen him. One member of Kemper's Brigade, who marched past Lee on the way to his position in line, recorded in his journal that he was unsettled by Lee's demeanor. "I must confess that the General's face does not look as bright as tho' he were certain of success," wrote John Dooley.[23]

By contrast, the always high-strung Pickett started the day in jaunty spirits over this rare opportunity to get into combat and play the leading role in Lee's plans. He envisioned his division as being hand-picked by Lee to occupy the place of honor in a grand assault with practically the entire army advancing in coordination all along the line. This would not be the vicious close in-fighting of Seven Pines and Gaines' Mill the previous spring, but more like Napoleon's Old Guard sweeping everything before it on the broad plains of Belgium. What an image: George Pickett leading the Army of Northern Virginia into battle! He may not have heard these words from General Lee's mouth, but he had it on good authority that this was the plan.[24] By early afternoon however, his initial euphoria had worn off, to be replaced by a sense of growing gloom and foreboding. The more he thought about it the more it seemed he was not the lucky commander of an irresistible assault but the victim of a hopeless charge.[25]

The assault finally moved forward a little after 3:00 p.m. with Pickett clearly identifiable at the head of his troops.[26] Lee selected as his spot to watch the assault the low ground just back of the foremost Confederate batteries (where the Virginia monument stands today). On that afternoon it was an artillery and reserve area. There he sat quietly on his favorite horse Traveller, with members of his staff around him. What happened in the next forty-five minutes, however, is the subject of considerable confusion and controversy. At the center of the controversy is George Pickett. His personal role in the assault has been greatly overblown by calling it "Pickett's Charge." His division was one of three assigned to take part in the main assault (the others were Henry Heth's, and Dorsey Pender's), drawn from two corps (the First and Third). The men of Pickett's Division constituted only about one-third of the roughly 14,000 troops assigned.

They advanced smartly and resolutely from their jumping-off place. At the Emmitsburg Road, Pickett gave his only significant order of the day, directing them to oblique left to point toward the angle in the stone wall that was their objective and to bring them into closer alignment with the divisions of James Pettigrew and Isaac Trimble. Robert Garnett, James Kemper, and Lewis Armistead took personal charge of the men as they crossed the road and pushed onward. Casualties mounted alarmingly, including Garnett and Kemper, until by the time they reached the stone wall, Armistead was the last senior officer still standing and urging the men to close with the enemy. Thus inspired, a relative handful broke through the Union lines and held their objective briefly before being driven back at great slaughter. Later, when they had time to think about it, a feeling of intense bitterness grew up among both officers and men that they had not been "supported" as they should have been, and from that point it became easy to seek scapegoats for what happened. Among other divisions in the army, there were even some who dared to criticize Lee himself for sending the Virginians to

Library of Congress, Washington, D.C.

"High Tide at Gettysburg" from an imaginative drawing by C.S. Reinbar. First appeared in Scribner's Magazine, *July, 1903.*

be "shot down like dogs." But no such heresy attached itself to Pickett's men, who, by all accounts, were still ready to follow Marse Robert anywhere.[27]

As the shell-shocked survivors of Pickett's Division returned to their lines, they did not retrace the zig-zag course they had followed in advancing nearly a mile diagonally across the field. Instead, they took the shortest way back, "along the extremity of Seminary Hill [Ridge], not far from the spot selected by Lee for watching the battle."[28] This meant that the commanding general of the army was one of the first officers they met when they got back to their lines.

By all rights, Pickett's Charge should have been a sentence of death for the man who led it. But it wasn't, and no one was more surprised by that than George Pickett himself. His lame explanation that it was a "miracle" he himself survived did not begin to answer all the questions. The seeds of controversy were planted on the battlefield itself. Somewhere in the open expanse of field and farm between Cemetery Ridge and Seminary Ridge, he disappeared from sight, or at least from the historical record. The mystery, quite simply, is where was General Pickett during the climax of Pickett's Charge, and it is at the heart of the Lee-Pickett relationship. The numerous eyewitness accounts are confusing and contradictory. What is known is that he rode into the Charge, and when it was over he came out unscathed. Every other officer in his division who got anywhere near the stone wall atop Cemetery Ridge was either killed or wounded.[29] At the climax of the assault, with his men leaderless, Pickett was apparently "missing in action." It did not matter where he was; his absence was conspicuous, and the questions were first raised not in the minds of historians many years removed, but in the minds of his fellow officers in the Army of Northern Virginia.[30]

It is impossible to imagine such a controversy attaching itself to Lee, not because of some untouchable mythology that surrounds Marse Robert, but because of the very real evidence provided by the two or three famous "Lee to the rear!" episodes a year later, when he rode into the front lines to personally lead a counter-attack and save the day. On both occasions, first at the Wilderness (May 6, 1864) and then at Spotsylvania (May 10 and 11, 1864), hundreds of men witnessed his impetuous action and forcibly prevailed upon him to take his proper place in the rear of the army. "Lee to the rear!" and "For God's sake, General, go back!" became rallying cries for his adoring soldiers. Thus inspired by his example, they drove the enemy back. As staff officer A. L. Long later described one of the moments, "It had become a question of victory or defeat, and any general may excusably expose himself when the fate of a battle hangs upon a thread." Lee himself once told Jefferson Davis after the latter had chided him for exposing himself unnecessarily, that he "could not understand things well unless he saw them." As Davis put it, "In the excitement of battle his natural combativeness would sometimes overcome his habitual self-control."[31]

Unknown artist, *Memoirs of Robert E. Lee* by A.L. Long (1886).

"General Lee to the Rear!" This dramatic moment in the Wilderness testified to Lee's personal courage, even foolhardiness, when the occasion demanded. No one ever recorded such an inspiring moment in George Pickett's career.

No such vivid memories have survived of a heroic George Pickett at the forefront of the assault on July 3. Not a single Confederate enlisted man or officer ever stepped forward to say that George Pickett was present at the stone wall when the battle was hanging in the balance. By consensus, the most inspiring general officer on the field that day was Brigadier General Lewis Armistead, who with his hat on his sword led the last desperate push over the stone wall, giving up his life in a final hopeless, frantic attempt to win the objective. One can argue that major generals are not supposed to be in the front ranks during an attack, and the same argument applies to commanding generals of armies, but that did not stop Lee in the Wilderness. One can also argue that some general officers, such as A. P. Hill, possessed what amounted to a suicidal impulse for reasons unconnected to their military duties which led them to take unnecessary risks. It is true that Southern culture placed an unnaturally high premium on personal valor irrespective of rank. We turn once more to A. L. Long to provide the best explanation of Lee's personal code on the battlefield: "He never exposed himself recklessly or unnecessarily," said Long, "though no consideration of personal safety ever deterred him from the full performance of the duties which necessarily devolve upon a commanding general."[32] What were Lee's minimal standards of personal bravery for his officers? He never said, but his actions indicate that they were somewhere between foolhardiness and simple self-preservation. This leaves unanswered the question of whether Pickett's presence (and likely death) at the stone wall would have made the slightest difference in the outcome of Pickett's Charge. Probably not, any more than Lee charging out of the woods like Philip Sheridan at Winchester would have had a similar effect in turning the men around who were fleeing for safety. But the fact is, nobody questioned Lee's personal behavior on that bloody afternoon, while many people raised questions about George Pickett's. In any event, a one-to-one correlation of Pickett at Gettysburg versus Lee at the Wilderness or Spotsylvania is superficial and unfair. There is no way to judge Lee's opinion of Pickett's courage in the absence of Lee's own words, and on that count Lee was completely silent.

The two can be fairly judged, however, on the basis of their public behavior on the afternoon of July 3. Those who observed both men were struck by the difference in their reaction to the disaster of Pickett's Charge. The first officer to whom Pickett spoke, Lieutenant Francis W. Dawson of Longstreet's staff, wrote later of how the general was crying bitter tears over the loss of his division even as frantic staff officers were running around trying to rally the men. In the same paragraph Dawson describes what an inspiration Lee was in those same moments, "communing with the angels of heaven."[33] The contrast is striking.

Another in a position to compare the battlefield leadership of both Lee and Pickett was Lieutenant Colonel Arthur Fremantle of Her Majesty's Coldstream Guards, who was present that day as an unofficial military observer for the British army. Like Dawson, Fremantle was impressed by Lee's stoic demeanor in the face of the disaster. He watched Lee call upon the men "to bind up [their] hurts and take up a musket in this emergency," and marveled that "very few failed to answer his appeal." The Englishman did not remember specifically seeing George Pickett in action that afternoon, but he heard some of Pickett's men as "they spoke in admiration of the advance of [the] division, and of the manner in which Pickett himself had led it." Some others would later question whether Pickett had in fact been at the front or somewhere in the rear during the advance, but for Fremantle there was no doubt that Pickett had done his duty.

One who spoke to Pickett personally was Major W.T. Poague of the Confederate artillery who was posted in the front lines. He spoke with both Lee and Pickett in the space of a few minutes as the broken remnants of Pickett's Charge streamed back into Confederate lines. Pickett rode up first, accompanied by neither staff nor enlisted men. He was, as Poague remembered, distraught and incapable of issuing orders, responding to Poague's repeated requests for orders by gazing off intently toward the smoke over Seminary Ridge. On his face, Poague observed, was "an expression of pain and sadness." His only acknowledgment that Poague was even on the same field was a bit of grim advice: "I think you had better save your guns;" then he rode off without waiting for a response. No orders were issued and no help was offered by the division commander to the anxious artillery officer.

Just a few moments later Lee rode up to Poague's position. In the cauldron of battle the commanding general had apparently recovered from his earlier attack of anxiety. Now Poague could not help but notice Lee's cool, businesslike manner even as the army was in chaos around him. A brief conversation ensued, which Lee opened with a question about the condition of Poague's Battery: "How are you off for ammunition, Major?" To Poague's answer that he had some and had issued orders to bring up more, Lee replied, "Ah! that's well. We may need them."[34]

Among the many chroniclers of that day, Poague offers the best study of two contrasting personalities at a single crucial moment. The same contrast that Poague, and to a lesser extent Dawson, noted that afternoon must have been apparent to other officers on the field. More importantly, they must have been apparent to Lee himself as he fought to hold his army together. The disapproval Poague felt for Pickett compared to his admiration for Lee is palpable in his account.

Moments later, in a more famous encounter, Lee and Pickett crossed paths, a chance meeting that only occurred because Lee was in the front lines to observe the action and Pickett's Division had fallen back in a straight line from the angle. Present at that moment was Captain R. A. Bright of Pickett's staff, who watched in fascination as the two men came face to face. Meeting his commanding general caused the highly emotive Pickett to burst into renewed tears. Lee spoke to his division commander first, addressing him in "a slow and distinct manner." Said Lee: "Place your division in the rear of this hill, and be ready to repel the advance of the enemy should they follow up their advantage."

Pickett's reply came back charged with bitterness: "General Lee, I have no division now! Armistead is down, Garnett is down, and Kemper is mortally wounded."

To this Lee responded with soothing words: "Come, General Pickett, this has been my fight, and upon my shoulders rests the blame. The men and officers of your command have written the name of Virginia as high as it has ever been written before." While addressing him, Lee stepped close and grasped Pickett's hand in a tender handshake, as he was wont to do with his officers on such highly charged occasions, something they never considered either demeaning or patronizing. Those watching were convinced that Lee felt "the repulse and slaughter of the division" as deeply as George Pickett.[35]

Lee may have been taken aback by Pickett's outburst, but could hardly have been thrown off balance. He had confronted angry, highly emotional officers before, and under similar circumstances. After the Battle of Antietam the previous September, he had inquired of John Bell Hood, "Great God, General Hood, where is the splendid division you had this morning?"

"They are lying on the field where you sent them, sir," Hood replied bitterly. "My division has been almost wiped out!"[36]

Now a similar scenario was unfolding at Gettysburg which demanded all of Lee's tact and forbearance. Recriminations aside, Lee on this occasion had also issued a direct order to Pickett about where to place his division. If Pickett made any acknowledgment that he had just received a direct order from his commanding general, it is not recorded. What Lee knew, and what Pickett should have known had he not been so distraught, was that Pickett did indeed still have a division. It was decimated and disorganized but still capable of being led, and Lee expected no less of him. The brief conversation ended when Lee turned to speak to some wounded men who were passing by. For his part, Pickett rode dejectedly back to Pitzer's Run where the remnants of his division—no more than three to four hundred at this point—were gathering to slake their thirst and bathe their wounds.[37]

Despite Moxley Sorrel's unequivocal assertion years later that "no man failed [Lee] that day," the record shows that George Pickett was not the only officer unhinged by the slaughter that occurred in front of Cemetery Ridge. His West Point classmate and old friend Cadmus Wilcox was also practically beside himself and for the same reason—much of his command lay dead or wounded on the field at the end of the battle. Wilcox and Pickett had shared a drink and wished each other good luck shortly before the charge, and now they found themselves in the same boat when it was over. The ever-present Arthur Fremantle saw Wilcox come up to General Lee, "and explain, almost crying, the state of his brigade." Lee used the same earnest, supplicating tone with Wilcox that he had with Pickett, grasping his hand and telling him with forced cheerfulness, "Never mind, General, all this has been my fault—it is I who have lost this fight, and you must help me out of it in the best way you can."

Unlike Pickett, Wilcox did not rage back at the old man standing before him, but whether he was one of those who were, in Fremantle's words, "encouraged and reanimated," is unclear. It may have been Wilcox and Pickett that Fremantle had in mind when he wrote later that "very few failed to answer his appeal"—

a subtle but significant distinction from Moxley Sorrel's blanket testimonial (above).[38]

Since Lee practically ignored Pickett in his official reports of the Gettysburg campaign, it is impossible to know what he thought of his troublesome lieutenant's performance of July 3. Judging by the number of Pickett's fellow officers who later commented about his strange disappearing act at the climax of the battle, it is hard to believe that Lee was not aware of the rumors circulating afterwards.

The real question therefore is, did Lee believe those rumors? He had already showed that long before July 3 he had serious doubts about Pickett's reliability, which only confirmed the concerns felt around First Corps headquarters where Pickett's shortcomings were well known. It is safe to say that if Longstreet and his staff had doubts about his favorite division commander, then Lee was not likely to be unaware of them. But to discover what Lee thought, we must examine what part Pickett played in the scheme of things after July 3, 1863. For better or for worse, George Pickett's future with the Confederate army was firmly in Robert E. Lee's hands.

5 Of Reports and Prisoners and Other Matters

On the long retreat back home, Pickett's Division was assigned the unheroic job of guarding some 3,500 Union prisoners all the way to Winchester, Virginia. General Lee issued the retreat orders on July 4, which said in part, "General Longstreet's corps will be charged with the escort of the prisoners, and will habitually occupy the center of the line of march."[1] Subsequent orders assigned the chore of escorting the Federal captives to Pickett's Division. This meant that they went with the wagon train and ambulances ahead of everybody else, which was the safest place to be on retreat, if not the most desirable. It also meant that they had to secure the river crossings at the Potomac and prepare Winchester for the arrival of the rest of the army. But even this relatively modest duty seemed too much for Pickett. He performed lethargically, even sullenly, unmotivated by Lee's July 4 orders exhorting every officer to exert "the utmost vigilance, steadiness, and boldness during the whole march."[2]

Pickett's mood during the retreat was as black as the Pennsylvania mud that the army was forced to march through. To begin with, he seemed to have taken quite literally his anguished outburst on the field at Gettysburg: "General Lee, I have no division!" When he wrote LaSalle five days after the battle he told her, "My division is almost extinguished," choosing to overlook the fact that he still had roughly 3,000 men in the ranks.[3] Yet he abdicated his command responsibilities by allowing his stragglers and walking wounded to roam at will through the army, making no effort to whip the shell-shocked troops into any sort of fighting shape.

Meanwhile, he continued to pester army headquarters for the return of Montgomery Corse's Brigade, and demanded to know how and when his shattered division was to be rebuilt. He also took the highly unorthodox measure of placing all his Union prisoners "on their honor," allowing them "equal liberties with my own soldier boys." His generosity went beyond mere humanitarian concern. In cavalier fashion, he advised his charges to, "enjoy themselves the best they could." As for the Union officers, he had his adjutant and inspector general turn them loose on their solemn promise to report to Richmond "if they were not duly [paroled] by their government." None of these arrangements were approved by the commanding general, nor met with his approval when he learned of them.[4]

On the contrary, Pickett's peevish behavior and poor attitude on the way home from Gettysburg led to a testy exchange of letters with army headquarters. Pickett himself initiated the correspondence on July 7 by questioning his marching orders and raising again the old issue of his missing brigades.[5] In the next two days an exasperated Lee fired back three letters filled with detailed instructions and stinging rebuke to his self-willed major general. "I regret that you did not send on the Federal officers with the guard assigned them," he wrote on July 9, before proceeding to lay out in the most precise language the way he wanted the prisoners handled. Chastised but hardly repentant, Pickett wrote LaSalle, "Unfortunately, I was not permitted to release [the Union officers] at this point, and they were required to march with the rest of the prisoners."[6]

On the surface, the "humiliating" prisoner escort duty was the thing that most rankled Pickett, and he was not shy in expressing his displeasure to General Lee. He could hardly have failed to note that his "brave Virginians" had gone full circle, from bringing up the rear of the army on the advance to being the vanguard in the retreat, the exact opposite of traditional military etiquette, which considered the "post of honor" to be at the front of an advance or assault and at the rear during a retreat. The placement of his division naturally provoked questions in Pickett's mind. Had Lee lost confidence in them? Were they to be reassigned to permanent garrison or guard duty as soon as the army was safe on Virginia soil?

He also could hardly have been unaware of Alfred Iverson's downfall: his brigade taken away, assigned to provost guard duty, and ultimately relieved of duty entirely for his behavior on July 1. Did Pickett imagine these things happening to himself next? Escorting prisoners and rounding up stragglers and deserters were two duties of a kind, and it was well known that Iverson too had been emotionally shattered by his experience at Gettysburg. A man much less sensitive than George Pickett might easily see disturbing parallels in their fates at the hands of General Lee. It was like waiting for the other shoe to fall. Even before the official word came down, "scuttlebutt" in the army had already decided the fate of Alfred Iverson.[7]

Pickett demanded some answers and Lee responded in a remarkably contrite letter of July 9. "It was with reluctance that I imposed upon your gallant division the duty of conveying prisoners to Staunton [*sic.*]," he wrote. Then, rather than put Pickett in his place for presuming to question rightful orders, Lee patiently explained the reasons behind those orders. He also subtly reminded the major general of where his priorities should be when he stated that everything that had been done was "the best for the public service."

The prisoner escort issue between the two men masked Pickett's deeper feelings of mortification and resentment over the disastrous assault of July 3. He wrote to LaSalle a few days afterwards about, "the unnecessary sacrifice" of his men, and told her how he had been "assured" that General Lee had ordered every brigade in the army "to charge Cemetery Hill [*sic.*]." In his own mind he was certain, "If I had only had my other two brigades a different story would have been flashed to the world." And in the end he wondered, "if in the light of the Great Eternity we shall any of us feel this was for the best and shall have learned to say, 'Thy will be done.'" Pickett's scriptural reference to the Heavenly Father ("Thy will be done") might just as easily have referred to the Father of the Army of Northern Virginia, whom he assured LaSalle, "all [of us] love, honor, and adore."[8]

Nothing signifies their different perspectives on the subject of duty more than the simple matter of what was "for the best." Pickett always thought first of what was best for George Pickett; Lee thought in terms of what was best "for the service." They could wear the same uniform and fight for the same cause, but this profound difference would always be between them. The son can love, honor, and adore the father, but still be unable to relate to him.

Lee took the high road in treating this latest chapter in their uneasy relationship as a division matter, not a personal rebuke. He took the unusual step of writing to Pickett personally rather than following his normal procedure of turning all official correspondence over to his adjutant Walter Taylor. He also failed to follow his usual procedure in dealing with recalcitrant officers. "When a man makes a mistake," he once explained, "I call him to my tent, talk to him, and use the authority of my position to make him do the right thing the next time."[9] Instead of a fatherly chat with Pickett, however, Lee preferred to communicate through written dispatches, a compromise perhaps between official correspondence through his staff and a face-to-face meeting.

Lee wanted to make sure Pickett understood that his latest duty assignment was not intended to degrade. "I regret that it has occasioned you and your officers any disappointment," he wrote soothingly. "I still have the greatest confidence in your division, and feel assured that, with you *at its head* [emphasis added], it will be able to accomplish any service upon which it may be placed." Pickett must know that he was not being lumped in the same category as Alfred Iverson, whose fate would become public knowledge in the next few days.[10]

Yet, if syntax offers any clue to Lee's thinking, his commendation of Pickett's Division first and then of its commander almost as an afterthought seems noteworthy. While he had practically unbounded faith in the soldiers of the Army of Northern Virginia, Lee was not so sure about some of their officers. "It would be unfortunate if I could not rely upon my division and brigade commanders [*i.e.*, to carry out their assigned duties]," he once remarked. And just a month before, in the midst of planning the Pennsylvania campaign, he had told John Bell Hood, "Our army would be invincible if it could be properly organized and officered. There never were such men in an army before. They will go anywhere and do anything if properly led."[11] In light of those statements, his soothing words to Pickett take on different meaning. The reassurance seems to be a classic case of why bring up something if there is really no problem. By denying the existence of any doubts about Pickett or his division, Lee seems to be acknowledging such doubts, or at least the rumors to that effect, which is just as bad for morale. There is no need to reassure where there is no doubt, no need to scotch rumors where there are no rumors. Throughout the rest of his post-

Gettysburg correspondence with Pickett, Lee seems to make a clear distinction between Pickett's Division and the leader of that division.

Lee's several missives to Pickett on the way back to Virginia also seem to reveal a fatherly sense of guilt associated with the slaughter of Pickett's Charge. "No one grieves more than I do at the loss suffered by your noble division in the recent conflict or honor it more for its bravery and gallantry," he wrote on July 9. "It will give me heartfelt satisfaction when an opportunity occurs, to do all in my power to recruit its diminished ranks and to reorganize it in the most efficient manner."[12] Lee was as good as his word. He wrote President Davis one month later that he planned to transfer the 49th Virginia from Early's Division to Pickett's, commenting, "This will strengthen Pickett a little and I believe will be agreeable to the regiment."[13]

Pickett's ambivalent feelings about the Great Charge and the orders behind it were first poured out in a series of letters to his fiancee written between July 4 and July 12. In one of his strongest statements to LaSalle Corbell, written two weeks after Gettysburg, he commented, "If the charge made by my gallant Virginians...had been supported, or even if my other two brigades...had been with me, we would now, I believe, have been in Washington, and the war practically over."[14] Apart from the military naivete of his thinking, this comment reveals a bitterness toward superiors who had failed to order up the necessary support for his charge, and who had also deprived him of two-fifths of his division before the battle was even joined. His two immediate superiors who put into motion the assault of July 3 were General Lee and First Corps commander James Longstreet. Since Longstreet was also his close personal friend and mentor, Lee by subtraction had to be the principal villain in this line of thinking. Longstreet never felt any estrangement from Pickett and defended him stoutly to the day he died. Writing his account of July 3, Old Pete described the mildest of reactions from his favorite major general: "The only thing Pickett said of his charge was that he was distressed at the loss of his command. He thought he should have had two of his brigades that had been left in Virginia; with them he felt that he would have broken the lines."[15]

Perhaps Pickett kept his true feelings to himself, or perhaps Longstreet was covering for him, as he had done numerous times before. If Pickett did not say very much openly, he expressed himself volubly when he sat down to write his official report, which eventually became a *cause celebre*. Most general officers liked to put off this duty as long as possible, but Pickett had things to get off his chest that would not wait. He was still seething with indignation and resentment when he wrote up his report while the army was enroute back to Virginia. We will probably never know precisely what that report said since it has been lost to history, but we know from Lee's reaction and from others who saw the report that it was unsparing in its approbation and recriminations. Longstreet must have agreed with its conclusions because, as Pickett's corps commander, he would have had to sign off on it before it reached Lee. Longstreet himself had strongly criticized Lee's decisions on July 3, but those criticisms were not done in such a way as to become part of the official record. The contents of Pickett's report would go on the record, thus furnishing a rich field for political troublemakers and journalistic pettifoggers back home.

Ordinarily, Lee studiously avoided reading after-action reports, leaving it to his staff to peruse and forward them to Richmond. Walter Taylor, Lee's adjutant, never presented routine communications to the commanding general unless they were "of decided importance and of a nature to demand his judgment and decision."[16] Apparently, with Pickett's report, Taylor saw all sorts of red flags, and decided to break the unofficial headquarters rule and put it before Lee. That fact alone suggests that the severity of Pickett's rhetoric overstepped the bounds of propriety.

While we know the gist of the report, *i.e.*, criticism of fellow officers, we do not know what names were named or what troops were specifically faulted. And we can only guess from Lee's response, which is part of the official record, how intemperate the language was that Pickett used. The timing of the report is significant. Pickett wrote it while still in high dudgeon over having to escort Union prisoners. He had only to review Lee's recent correspondence on that score to rekindle his indignation.

The temper of Pickett's after-action report is not surprising, nor is Lee's response. The commanding general returned the offending report, asking Pickett to destroy both the original and any copies, and in their place to substitute one confining itself "to casualties only." Pickett obligingly destroyed the original, "in accordance with Lee's wishes," but never submitted a replacement.[17] Whether this was out of personal pique or mere negligence we cannot say, but Lee did not press the matter. The next time he asked Pickett for an official report was April 10, 1865, to cover his division's operations "from the time of the recent attack of the enemy near Petersburg to the present." That request was met promptly and without disputation, though the tone was quite peevish and reproachful.[18]

While the rejection of Pickett's battle report was in nowise a personal condemnation of its author, that was the only way Pickett could take it, given his temperament and his feelings at the time. He was thin-skinned, and his nerves had been stretched to the breaking point as a result of what he had endured at Gettysburg. Add to that volatile mixture the written scoldings administered by Lee on the retreat, and it is no wonder that Pickett felt he was being persecuted by his commanding general when his report came back with what amounted to an "unsatisfactory grade." He had never learned to hold his tongue, and his pen was an extension of that sharp tongue. Although Pickett did not say it, he probably would have seconded Colonel Walter Taylor's complaint about their general-in-chief: "I never worked so hard to please any one, and with so little effect as with General Lee. He is so *unappreciative* [emphasis in original]." Like Taylor and countless others who longed to please Marse Robert and win his approval almost more than they wanted to whip the Yankees, Pickett thought Lee could be "so unreasonable and provoking at times," and George Pickett was a man easily provoked.[19]

Most officers were prudent enough to censor personal recriminations from their after-action reports, particularly following a bitter defeat. No officer wanted to be known as a curmudgeon and a back-stabber; that reputation had helped speed the exit of D.H. Hill from the Army of Northern Virginia the previous year. Far better to follow the timeless dictum, "If you can't say something nice about someone, say nothing at all." This was the wise course of action followed by Cadmus Wilcox in writing his report of the battle, though he had plenty to complain about. He was thoroughly disgusted with the lack of support from Dick Anderson on July 2, but he refrained from criticizing the Third Corps division commander "lest my motives might have been misunderstood." Instead, Wilcox showed himself to be a true team player when he took up the pen on July 17, not even mentioning Anderson in his report. It was not until two years later when asked by Lee to recall his part in the battle that he cut loose with a denunciation of Anderson and others, stating, "I may wrong General A[nderson], but I always believed that he was too indifferent to his duties at Gettysburg."[20]

Pickett would have been much better off if, like Wilcox, he had filed a *pro forma* report and held his tongue until after the war, but he was too impetuous and far too angry to consider the consequences. He had seized the first opportunity that came along to vent his wrath and assign blame when what Lee really expected was something more like a whitewash than an inquest. The former was the approach Lee himself took in composing his official account of the campaign.

Lee's account of Gettysburg was written in two editions, the first dated July 31, 1863, and the second dated January, 1864. He described the advance into Pennsylvania, the climactic battle at Gettysburg, and the retreat to the line of the Rapidan in some detail. The second edition was more expansive because he was able to incorporate the reports of his various commanding officers, thereby speaking "more particularly of the conspicuous gallantry and good conduct of both officers and men." His guilelessness, compassion, and personal accountability shine through in both reports. He was generous in his praise and sparing in his criticisms. This generosity toward erring subordinates, of whom there were many, was so remarkable that it elicited dismay from his military secretary, Colonel Charles Marshall. Lee however explained to Marshall that he did not want his statements to "affect others injuriously," without specifying precisely who those "others" might be.[21]

On the subject of George Pickett and his role in the Gettysburg campaign, Lee is strangely silent in both reports. To be sure, "Pickett's Charge" was largely a creation of the Old Dominion public relations juggernaut, but one would still expect to find the leader of that proud division prominently mentioned in the commanding general's reports. Instead, Pickett is described as arriving on the battlefield late on July 2 with his three brigades to "re-enforce" Longstreet; after that, all the focus of Lee's very brief description of Pickett's Charge is on the Confederate troops. Lee praises those troops effusively—"[their] conduct was all that I could desire or expect"—but the man who led those troops is virtually a nonentity in Lee's version of things. In handing out personal plaudits, Lee named numerous "brave officers and patriotic gentlemen" who had faithfully discharged their duties, right down to quartermasters and inspectors-general. Even the tragically tardy Stuart had performed "valuable service" with his cavalry once they arrived on the scene. But not George Pickett. As a further irony, Lee passed over the division commander while singling out the brigade commanders, Garnett, Armistead, and Kemper, for commendation.[22]

It is a fact of the military system that careers can be made or broken by being mentioned in a commander's report. Promotions, medals, and public acclaim are often at stake. Reading Lee's account, it is as if the noble "Virginia division" had been commanded by some mysterious phantom on that historic afternoon.

Lee also did something else that was entirely unexpected yet completely in character after Gettysburg: he offered his resignation to Jefferson Davis. He made the magnanimous offer on August 8, soon after reaching the safe soil of Virginia and not long after chastising Pickett for provoking controversy with his ill-considered accusations. Lee began his letter to the president by citing a truism in the military business: "The general remedy for the want of success in a military commander is his removal." He referred vaguely to feelings of "discontent" with his leadership in the army, saying, "My brother officers have been too kind to report it, and so far the troops have been too generous to exhibit it." To pull the army together and restore confidence in its leadership, he offered himself as the sacrificial goat. Davis promptly refused to accept his resignation and encouraged him to fight on, reassuring him that he had the full confidence of not just the country but of the whole country.[23]

Within the army at least, no one was willing to go on record as calling for Lee's ouster. Even Pickett, for once, was wise enough not to air his grievances with his superiors. After the battle, Lee's staff closed ranks around him, attempting to shift the blame for the disaster onto others. They acted without Lee's connivance, but with the best of intentions, despite his repeated insistence, "It all rests upon me." Fingers were pointed in particular at Longstreet and Stuart.[24]

George Pickett got off scot-free when the accusations started flying because it was obvious he had played no part in either conceiving or planning the climactic assault of July 3, much less the operations of the previous two days. Lee probably saved him from some embarrassing questions when he stated in his report that the assault was made "under Longstreet's direction," and Longstreet noted that Lee "gave no orders or suggestions after his early designation of the point for which the column should march [*i.e.*, the center of the Union lines on Cemetery Ridge]."[25] That sort of absolution deflected any criticism from Pickett early on. Years later however, when questions did begin to come out about Pickett's role in the charge named for him, his staff, like Lee's, rallied in defense of their chief, writing a series of open letters to the Richmond newspapers and making other public statements absolving him of any and all blame for Gettysburg.[26]

6 The Exile That Wasn't Really

Whether Pickett was in Lee's bad graces after Gettysburg is a moot point. The only other officer from the battle who might usefully be compared to George Pickett was Brigadier General Alfred Iverson who had commanded a brigade of North Carolinians in Robert Rodes' Division on July 1. When his brigade was virtually snuffed out by the Union First Corps on the first day, Iverson "went to pieces and became unfit for further command." Later, in writing his official report, he tried unsuccessfully to deflect the blame, but upon their return to Virginia, Lee pushed to have him brought before a court martial. Jefferson Davis scotched that idea, "much to Lee's intense displeasure," so the commanding general had to be content with ousting Iverson from the Army of Northern Virginia. On the way home from Gettysburg, however, the disgraced general's brigade was taken away from him and he was assigned to provost marshal duty, a public degradation that everyone understood. Of all the general officers who could be said to have failed Lee at Gettysburg, only Iverson was called to answer for it, and even he escaped censure in Lee's official reports.[1]

By contrast, Pickett hardly suffered the same sort of shame and humiliation as Iverson, but his position in Lee's official family changed measurably. Superficially, nothing seemed to have changed. He retained command of his old Virginia division until very nearly the end of the war, although the brigades of that division were split up and scattered to the four winds. He was even given two opportunities for independent command—the first at New Berne, North Carolina, in 1864, then a year later at Five Forks, Virginia—which was indeed ironic. Successful independent command has always required an officer who sees the big picture, is self-assured, and seizes responsibility with delight. But that description hardly fit George Pickett, whose self-confidence had been shattered and whose professional skills had long been suspect.

Pickett was punished not with exile but with a diminished role in the Army of Northern Virginia. Lee, as the old joke goes, could not live with Pickett and could not live without him. Experienced combat officers were hard to come by in the best of times, and Pickett's "resumé" was still one of the most impressive in the army. Yet, as general officers continued to fall by the wayside for various reasons during the last twenty months of the war, Pickett was repeatedly passed over for promotion to corps commander—this despite his West Point training and battlefield experience. Other men who were colonels with Pickett at the beginning of the Civil War—including Richard Ewell, A. P. Hill, and John Bell Hood—rose to corps command or higher before the end. Pickett was never promoted again after he made major general in the fall of 1862. Douglas Southall Freeman once pointed out that, "Lee never hesitated and seldom erred in giving new stars to his worthy lieutenants," but added that, "Lee would not raise men whose ability he questioned."[2] Since Lee was Pickett's senior commanding officer during this entire time, he would have been the one to make the necessary recommendations for or against promotion. And any recommendation from Lee would hardly have been disregarded in Richmond.

Two of the most telling snubs of Pickett came in the first half of 1864. In January, when Jefferson Davis was casting about for another officer to take over the sputtering Confederate operations in West Virginia, he asked Lee for recommendations. At the time Pickett was unhappy in department command at Petersburg, and Lee was trying to ease Robert F. Hoke into that position. On January 27, Lee reviewed practically his entire roster of senior brigadier and major generals for Davis, saying, "There are many capable officers in this army," but he did not even mention Pickett's name. Then on May 7, the day after Longstreet was severely wounded at the Wilderness, Lee was forced to hurriedly reshuffle his officers to find a *temporary* replacement for the stalwart Longstreet. Lee considered his available choices before quickly settling on three possibilities to take over the First Corps: Jubal Early, Edward Johnson, or Richard Anderson. Not only did Pickett not make the "short list," his name was not even brought up in the discussions between Lee and his advisors although on the basis of seniority alone he certainly deserved to be considered. On the day that Longstreet was wounded, Pickett was engaged south of the James River opposing Ben Butler. But he was hardly beyond reach of Lee's headquarters with the Army of Northern Virginia had his immediate return been desired. He could have been summoned in a matter of hours. Instead he was left at Bermuda Hundred until superseded by General Beauregard on May 12, his services not being considered essential in the great battles against Grant north of the James. In two instances when the army needed experienced leadership to plug a hole, Pickett was overlooked, and both times Lee had the authority to make the call.[3]

Even apart from these two pointed snubs, Pickett's situation with Lee and the Army of Northern Virginia was in limbo. He spent the fall of 1863 on detached duty south of Richmond, his brigades scattered, some to North Carolina and some to Charleston where they were attached to Beauregard's command. During this time Pickett's principal job was recruiting his depleted ranks while keeping an eye on one of the quieter sectors. But he occupied most of his time sniping with subordinates over such matters as the sending of communications through proper military channels and the proper way to fold and address official correspondence. The condition of his command reflected the mental disarray of its commander, and courts-martial of both men and officers were a frequent occurrence. Lee, keeping a long-distance eye on Pickett, chided him at least once "for bickering and controversy with other officers."[4] Tiring of the petty in-fighting, Lee finally informed the War Department that he preferred General Beauregard as head of the Department of North Carolina and Southern Virginia. Upon that recommendation Beauregard was transferred from Charleston on April 18, 1864, to take over the defenses of Richmond and its environs, thus further demoting Pickett from titular department head to district commander under Beauregard.

The two men's fates intersected again in early 1864 when Lee called for an attack on New Berne, North Carolina, a Federal stronghold which posed a threat to the Army of Northern Virginia's rear. Lee believed a successful attack would secure "much subsistance for the army" and at the same time "have the happiest effect in North Carolina and inspire the people."[5] Incorrectly as it turned out, he also believed the Federal garrison was ripe for the plucking.

Strictly speaking, New Berne was in Pickett's department, so he was the logical choice to organize such an attack, either leading it himself or designating a commander. But Lee preferred the job be given to young Robert F. Hoke, a brigadier general who had been inactive since Chancellorsville and who was familiar with that part of North Carolina. President Davis had more faith in George Pickett, however, and overruled Lee.[6] Hoke instead received the command of one of the three brigades in Pickett's attack force.

Lee's orders to Pickett on January 20, 1864, were to attack New Berne in conjunction with Confederate naval units. The wording of them was curious because they were so uncharacteristically precise for Lee, a commander who was notorious for his vague and open-ended orders. Moreover, traditional military doctrine has always held that a commander tells his subordinates what he wants done but not how to do it; trying to do otherwise robs the local commander of his initiative. Yet on this occasion Lee's orders to Pickett were precise to the point of being pedantic. Pickett was instructed how much and what kind of artillery to employ as well as the exact wording to be used in notifying General W.H.C. Whiting at Fort Fisher of the impending attack. Although Lee left the details of the plan and the final decision to go or not go up to Pickett's "good judgment," it was clear from the wording that he expected his lieutenant to follow the plan as outlined and do everything humanly possible to attain the objective. Finally, Lee urged him to use "secrecy, expedition, and boldness" in all his movements.[7]

Once again, Moxley Sorrel, Longstreet's chief of staff, provides the likliest explanation for Lee's uncharacteristically precise instructions: Longstreet "always made us give him [Pickett] things very fully...[and] stay with him to make sure he did not get astray."[8] Denied the commander he wanted, Lee was, at least, determined to see that Pickett did not "get astray."

The attack of February 1 failed miserably, a victim of poor coordination and complicated timing. Two days later Pickett gave up and pulled back first to his Kinston, North Carolina, jumping-off point, then to Goldsborough, North Carolina, and finally Petersburg. He had shot his bolt. In only the second battle report he had ever written for Lee (Gettysburg was the first),

Pickett blamed the setback on a variety of factors including his naval support, the terrain, and formidable Union defenses. But he assigned the lion's share of the blame to Brigadier General Seth Barton, saying, "I have but little doubt that had Barton pushed on we might have been successful." Perhaps having learned his lesson after Gettysburg, he tempered the tone of his criticism in the official report, but bluntly stated it in an accompanying cover letter which he sent to Lee. In the same letter, he practically pleaded with Lee for a measure of sympathy if not outright exoneration: "I am sorry nothing more was done...I hope, general, you will understand my reasons for the withdrawal."[9]

Lee never criticized Pickett directly for the New Berne defeat, even after reading Robert Hoke's shocking report that "surprise was most complete...the place was within our grasp. The work could have been done." With those words echoing in his mind and a real donnybrook threatening to erupt between Pickett and Barton, he sat down and wrote a personal note to Pickett saying, "I regret the failure to capture the place," and advising him that he was requesting a formal investigation by the War Department. Although Barton had made the original request and his reputation was at stake, a court of inquiry would certainly examine closely Pickett's role in the affair, and this could not have been displeasing to Lee. Before closing the book on New Berne, Lee also wrote a personal note to General Hoke praising him for his part in the work.[10]

The results of Lee's personal involvement in the New Berne expedition were mixed. He had proposed the attack originally, designated the troops to be used, tried to select the commander, and outlined the attack plan. When it failed, however, no measure of blame attached itself to him because he had not been the commander of record on the scene. Pickett, on the other hand, had to attack a strongly fortified town with subordinates he scarcely knew, according to a plan that was not his own, and dependent upon a naval contingent he did not control. Once again he had been a pawn in somebody else's plans. For unknown reasons the court of inquiry never convened. Perhaps Lee reconsidered or, more likely, there was neither the time nor the officers to spare for such bureaucratic shows.

A few weeks later Pickett proposed his own plan for operations in North Carolina. Lee commended him, called the plan "good" and encouraged him to "carry it into execution at once," but then took away the troops necessary to do so. Possibly anticipating the next point of Federal attack, however, he advised Pickett to look to his defenses at Petersburg: "They should be strengthened immediately to their fullest extent."[11]

Pickett never got a second chance in North Carolina. When another Confederate offensive was planned with the goal of retaking Plymouth, Washington, and New Berne, the man at the head was Robert Hoke, Lee's choice in the first place. Pickett was out of the loop on this one, but when he learned of the new operation he was reportedly still "anxious to conduct it in person."[12] On April 18, Hoke succeeded where Pickett had failed, driving the Federals out of one of their major coastal enclaves at Plymouth. For his victory he was promoted to major general and received the thanks of Jefferson Davis while Pickett continued to languish in garrison duty at Petersburg, neither entrusted with offensive operations in his own department nor recalled to the Army of Northern Virginia.

To date, Pickett's record with the Army of Northern Virginia since being promoted to major general had consisted of being in reserve at Fredericksburg, detached duty in southeast Virginia, a near annihilation at Gettysburg, failed independent command in North Carolina, and several official reprimands from the commanding general of the army. Since Gettysburg the only good thing that had happened to him was his marriage to LaSalle Corbell of Nansemond, Virginia, which took place on September 16, 1863, in Petersburg. He was granted unofficial leave by Longstreet for the occasion, despite active preparations by the First Corps at this time to move west and join the Army of Tennessee. Perhaps Old Pete knew that Pickett was not slated to rejoin the army in field operations any time soon.

Lee's considered opinion of the timing of this marriage is not known, although his earlier disapproval of Pickett's self-indulgent courting behavior had been well demonstrated. Some of the army's senior officers, Jubal Early and Eppa Hunton to name just two of the most outspoken, opposed wartime marriages as detrimental to the service. But Lee was no Puritan Covenantor or grumpy misogynist. He had a fondness for the young ladies and a deep romantic streak that few men were allowed to see. During the last days of the Confederacy, on the very day that he learned of the disaster at Five Forks, Lee granted permission for his faithful adjutant Walter Taylor to make a quick dash to

Richmond to marry his longtime sweetheart before the city fell to the Yankees.[13]

Lee could be as romantic and sentimental as the next fellow, but only after the demands of duty had been satisfied. What he had no patience for were men who slipped away from their duties without notifying their superiors in order to court the fairer sex. In this regard Lee was only reflecting the attitude of many leading Southerners who took a dim view of any officer too addicted to wine, women, and song. The popular attitude was evidenced in what the press said about Earl Van Dorn after that general officer was shot by a jealous husband in 1862: "He was never at his post when he ought to be. He was either tied to a woman's apron strings or heated with wine."[14] Lee would never have said such a thing about one of his officers, nor did he ever have any occasion to deal with Van Dorn in the command structure of the Confederate army. But he was well acquainted with George Pickett's pleasure-seeking ways, as was the rest of the army.

There is no reason to suspect that Lee was in any way opposed to George and LaSalle's marriage, especially since he and Mrs. Lee were invited to the ceremony. On the contrary, he may have seen it as a good thing for the service if it kept the ardent Pickett from trying to dash off at every opportunity to rendezvous with his inamorata. When the happy day came, many of the Confederacy's shining lights, among them President Davis, and Generals Longstreet and Stuart—but not Lee — were in attendance. Lee did bestow his blessing, in the form of a "beautiful fruitcake" sent as a wedding present "from the Robert E. Lee Family."[15]

Social gestures should never be mistaken for official approval however, as Pickett's status within the army proved once more. He did not accompany Longstreet out west with Hood and Lafayette McLaws. Nor did he stay with Lee and the Army of Northern Virginia as it maneuvered south of the Rappahannock looking for an opening to strike at the Army of the Potomac. Pickett remained in limbo south of the James until February 1864, when Longstreet returned from Tennessee and requested Pickett's Division be reunited with the First Corps. It is noteworthy that the desire to reconstitute the old First Corps and bring Pickett back to the Army of Northern Virginia originated not with Lee but with Longstreet. Once again, Longstreet's mentoring was the crucial element in keeping Pickett's career afloat. Lee, however, seemed in no hurry to comply with his favorite corps commander's simple request. He passed along Longstreet's request with a lukewarm endorsement, and did not protest too loudly when President Davis inquired, "How can Pickett's division be replaced [i.e., in southeast Virginia]?" Another two and a half months would pass before Pickett was finally ordered back to active operations with Lee's army.[16]

Before he could rejoin it, a new Federal threat in the form of the Army of the James landed at Bermuda Hundred, where the James and Appomattox rivers came together, and Pickett was pressed into service to "bottle up" Ben Butler. After Pickett saved Richmond and even accomplished the amazing feat of driving the Federals back from their Bermuda Hundred lines, Lee announced himself "delighted and grateful with the result." By coincidence, the commanding general had been nearby and witnessed Pickett's spirited attack against the superior force. He was so impressed he allowed himself a bit of uncharacteristic jocularity in his official dispatch when he spoke of his normally vexatious lieutenant: "We tried very hard to stop Pickett's men from capturing the breastworks of the enemy, but could not do it. I hope his loss has been small."[17] Moxley Sorrel, acting adjutant for Dick Anderson at the time, forwarded a copy of the dispatch to Pickett, who must have been pleased, though there is no record of his reaction to this off-handed praise. Soon thereafter, Pickett, his division, and the Army of Northern Virginia were all reunited in the siege lines around Petersburg.

For the first time in ten months, George Pickett was an integral part of Lee's army, being no longer on detached duty. That meant among other things that he was now Lee's problem again, not Richmond's as he had been when he was a department commander. But prolonged absence had not moderated his former predilection for complaining and fretting about anything and everything. He was no sooner assigned to A. P. Hill's Third Corps (May 20) than he began grumbling to headquarters that his marching orders were unclear and contradictory, returning the orders with the notation that he had "corrected" them himself. This confusion may explain why it took him five days to join Hill. In the same communique he bristled at the implication that he had been the least wayward in his movements.[18] He did not stay long with A. P. Hill, but was soon back with Longstreet's First Corps, a much more agreeable arrangement for all concerned.

Another bad habit he had not shaken was absenting himself from his command whenever he felt like it, as he had done in the winter and spring of 1863 while courting LaSalle. He continued to act as if he thought he was still with the pre-war army, when officers at distant frontier posts often took lengthy leaves of absence, which they extended almost at will without repercussion. But that was peacetime and this was wartime.

Even marriage and Lee's earlier reprimands could not clip Pickett's wings. When LaSalle gave birth to their first child in July 1864, the father was in the lines at Petersburg while mother and infant were in Richmond. He made immediate plans, as he informed her, to "fly to you both." The war would just have to wait. But he forgot to factor Lee into his plans. The Army of Northern Virginia's commander was no Longstreet when it came to granting leave willy-nilly or tolerating the practice of "french leave" by his officers. Pickett routinely applied to "the Great Tyee" for a pass, explaining, "My son was born this morning." To his surprise, Lee promptly rejected the application with this curt reminder: "Your country was born almost a hundred years ago." Not very historical but to the point. If he had been so inclined, Lee might also have added a little personal advice that had stood him in good stead all his life: Never "seek or receive indulgence from any one." When Pickett wrote LaSalle to explain why he would not be coming, he disingenuously claimed, "It was the first word suggestive of reproach that Marse Robert ever spoke to me," while admitting that, "He was right and I was reckless to ask."[19] Pickett's explanation was only half right, as the record shows.

By his constant complaining and alarmist reports Pickett had already put himself once more in Lee's bad graces in this campaign. At the end of May he informed headquarters in characteristic melodramatic fashion that his men did not have enough bread—no surprise there since the whole Confederate army was short of rations—and ended with the plea, "We must get something or the division will be worse than useless."[20] Ironically, this evaluation echoed the last inspection report, which had given the division a failing grade in virtually every performance category. In discipline and efficiency Pickett's Division was far below Lee's standards for the Army of Northern Virginia. Among other signs of a troubled command, the customary drills and inspections were no longer being carried out. Everything from "accommodations for the sick" to "religious exercises" was neglected.

Lee was concerned enough about the condition of the division to bring it to the attention of the one man who could appeal to Pickett's better side, James Longstreet. Using terms like "unsoldierly and unmilitary..., lax in discipline..., loose in military instruction...," Lee warned his First Corps commander that "unless the division and brigade commanders are careful and energetic, nothing can be accomplished." He even pinpointed the source of the problem: not the nerve-wracking siege, or the winter elements, or even the fact that the war was entering its fourth year; the source of the problem, said Lee, was that Pickett and his officers were not "sufficiently attentive to the men,...not informed as to their condition." Not taking care of his men was the most serious charge that could be leveled against an officer, more serious than lateness, poor administration, or even losing battles. Lee himself had lost battles, the mighty Stonewall had been late, and Jeb Stuart was not much of an administrator, but no one had ever accused them of not taking care of their men. Lee closed by showing a rare glimpse of the iron fist within the velvet glove before reverting to his customary gracious approach. "I desire you to correct the evils in Pickett's division...by every means in your power," he commanded Longstreet, then changed to a more conciliatory tone: "I beg that you will insist upon these points."[21]

This obscure dispatch shows that Lee kept well informed of George Pickett's conduct, likely through the army's grapevine as well as through regular inspection reports. By whatever means he got his information, he was troubled by what he heard. Racked with pain from heart and bowel problems, desperately casting about for some tactical move to re-take the initiative from Grant, Lee nonetheless took the time to reprove his most troublesome lieutenant. In characteristic fashion, he chose to do it indirectly.

Lee knew that the efficiency of any command is merely a reflection of its leadership. The lack of drill instruction, attention to clothing, and other failures noted by Lee bespoke deeper problems, mainly a lack of essential discipline throughout the command. There was no doubt where Lee stood when it came to discipline. He expressed himself strongly on the subject about this same time in a letter to President Davis: "The great want in our army is firm discipline," he wrote.[22] Two years before, to the month, Lee had specifically criticized Pickett's command on the same score, lack of discipline. While the fighting condition of the entire army had suffered since those heady days of early 1863, no other command had been censured by the commanding general in such blunt terms as Pickett's Division. Good discipline started at the top, and no troops could be expected to perform if their officers did not set a proper example.

Lee would return to this subject again and again. In August 1864, while trying to hold his army together in the siege lines at Petersburg, he wrote this to Jefferson Davis: "To succeed it is necessary to set the example, and this necessarily confines [officers] to their duties, their camp and mess, which is disagreeable and deprives them of pleasant visits and dinners, etc."[23] Whom Lee had in mind, if anyone in particular, he did not say, but just seven months later, he had good reason to recall these words following the events at Five Forks.

On one point Lee and Pickett were in complete agreement, and that was the evils of desertion. Odd that two men so different should find agreement on an issue about which there was so much room to disagree. But Pickett, like Stonewall Jackson, had no compunction about punishing deserters to the full letter of the law. At one point during the siege of Petersburg, he had more than one hundred of his men in the guard-house under sentence for being AWOL. This was remarkable enough to be the subject of comment in Richmond. The law called for execution, and this is probably what Pickett had in mind, but for a two-month period in the fall of 1864 deserters were being pardoned *en masse* by Jefferson Davis. John H. Reagan, who sat in the Confederate cabinet for four years as postmaster general, noted that Davis "never approved a single death sentence" among the countless cases that came across his desk for review. By 1864, even Lee was driven to admonish the Confederate president by writing, "Desertion is increasing in the army, notwithstanding all my efforts to stop it. I think a rigid execution of the law is a mercy in the end." Lee's comments were attached as an endorsement to a letter from Pickett making the same point.[24]

Pickett clearly made a distinction between his own romantic forays during happier times versus soldiers simply going "over the hill" with probably no intention of returning; therefore, he saw no irony in his own stand. For Lee, there was no contradiction between his own behavior and his stand on the issue. And if Jackson had been alive, he would have added his voice to theirs. Nevertheless, they got no sympathy from Jefferson Davis. The president sent back a biting reply that the subject of official reprieves was "not a proper subject for the criticism of a military commander."[25] Presumably this included both army commanders and major generals. The matter was closed.

Pickett's tough stand on deserters was not so much a sign of a firm hand as a symptom of a troubled command, and Lee's handling of the division reflected as much. By informal arrangement, he ignored the customary chain of command during the Petersburg siege to assume personal control over Pickett's Division, frequently by-passing Longstreet's headquarters and issuing orders directly to Pickett.[26] He used the division as what has sometimes been described as a "mobile reserve," but a more likely purpose behind the change was to put Pickett on an even shorter leash.[27] It was a deceptive arrangement that gave the appearance that Pickett was Lee's "fireman," which was true as far as it went. It also placed Lee in the uncomfortable position of having to rely on the mercurial Pickett whenever an emergency came up, such as plugging a hole in the line, organizing a local offensive, or blocking a Federal move around the flank. But experienced field officers were in short supply by this date, and Pickett had shown at Bermuda Hundred that, if nothing else, he could still be a fighting general. Plus, his troops were still some of the most respected in the army when serious fighting was to be done. The immediate effect for George Pickett was to remove him from under the watchful care of James Longstreet, but it also removed Longstreet as a buffer between Pickett and army headquarters.

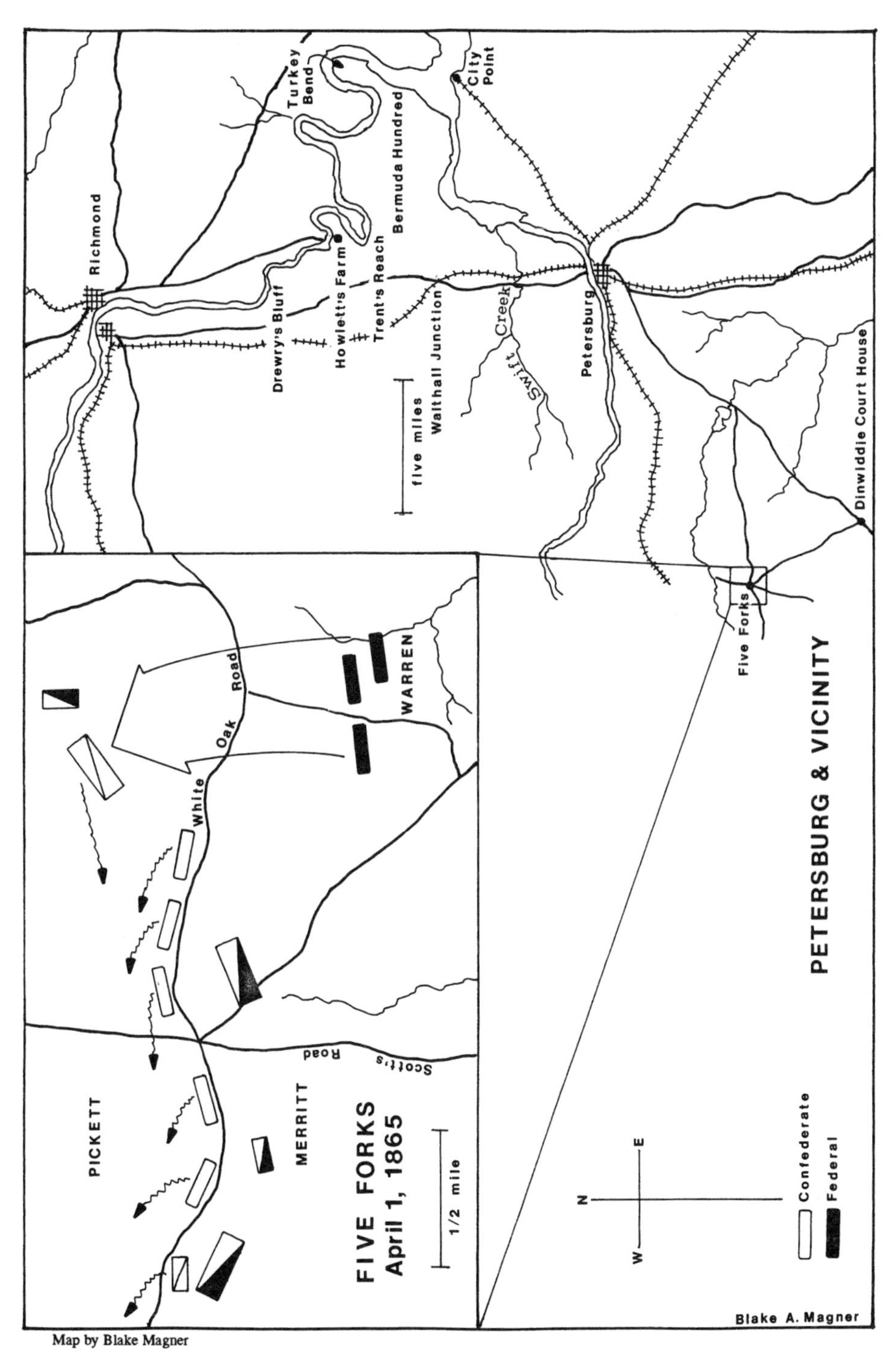

Map by Blake Magner

Five Forks

7 One Last Chance for Vindication

At the end of March 1865, Grant dispatched Philip Sheridan with 13,000 cavalry toward the western flank of the Confederate line to threaten the South Side Railroad, the last unbroken supply line out of Petersburg for the Confederates. The Second and Fifth Corps of the Union Army followed slowly in support.[1] Recognizing the seriousness of the threat, Lee's countermove was to scrape together five brigades (19,000 men) and dispatch them under Pickett to block Sheridan. Lee was so concerned with this new threat that he came over himself to "personally oversee the defence of his right flank," unwilling to entrust it to a major general.[2] On the morning of the 29th, the two men met ten miles west of Petersburg at Sutherland's Station, the somber commanding general and the nervous but eager-to-please major general. Here Lee outlined the threat and issued instructions which were uncharacteristically vague when dealing with George Pickett. Pickett's troops would be functioning as virtually an independent command, numbering almost one-third of the entire army once they were reinforced by elements of Fitz Lee's cavalry, and operating beyond the main lines with discretionary orders to meet Sheridan's threat as Pickett saw fit.

Lee was not dealing with Stonewall Jackson or Jeb Stuart here, both of whom were wizards at taking vague orders and discerning exactly what the commanding general wanted to accomplish. By March 1865 however, he was forced to entrust his plans to men like Matt Ransom, Henry Heth, Dick Anderson, John Pemberton—and George Pickett; with so much at stake he felt the need also to follow up on his initial orders. On the morning of the 30th, wearing what one observer described as "a black mackintosh and steeple white hat," he met once more with Pickett and the other four general officers to make his desired dispositions absolutely clear. They held an impromptu war council at Gravelly Run Creek, with Lee sitting on a broken fence and the others gathered closely around him, huddled against the cold rain. The commanding general used a stick to outline his plans in the mud, addressing each man in turn to make sure he understood his assigned position. This may have been the occasion when Lee emphasized to Pickett the importance of holding Five Forks against all odds; the exact words spoken on this occasion were not recorded. After an hour the council broke up and Pickett rode off to get his brigades moving.[3]

By the next morning all of Pickett's assigned brigades were on the right flank of the Petersburg lines, ready to advance south, past Five Forks and close with Sheridan at Dinwiddie Court House. With an initial numerical advantage of about 3:2, Pickett drove the surprised Federals well south of Dinwiddie and was on the verge of routing his opponent entirely when night fell. However, Sheridan had already called on Grant for infantry reinforcements, and as a result Gouverneur K. Warren's Fifth Corps was on the way. At the end of the day, Pickett suddenly got an attack of nerves and ordered his men back to their starting lines at Five Forks, five miles from Dinwiddie Court House, and about four miles west of Lee's right flank. Pickett suspected the same thing Sheridan had already seen when that Union officer confidently told a visitor from Grant's headquarters, "This force [Pickett's] is in more danger than I am. If I am cut off from the Army of the Potomac, it is cut off from Lee's army, and not a man in it should ever be allowed to get back to Lee!"[4]

At 2:00 a.m. on April 1, Pickett notified Lee, after the fact, of his decision to break off the engagement and retreat, citing as his reasons that he was badly outnumbered plus the dangerous gap that existed between his own force and the rest of the Confederate line. He also, as he later recollected events, called for reinforcements and a diversionary attack to relieve the mounting pressure on his front.

When Lee received the news of Pickett's precipitous withdrawal, he expressed open surprise at this sudden turn of events, and promptly sent a message back to Pickett reminding him how important Five Forks was "as the shield to the Southside road [*sic*] and key to the entire position [around Petersburg]." In words that would come back to haunt both men, Lee practically pleaded to, "Hold Five Forks at all hazards." Then he added this mild reproof: "regret exceedingly your forced withdrawal, and your inability to hold the advantage you had gained."[5]

Lee's explicit orders to hold Five Forks placed Pickett in a very awkward position, both literally and figuratively. It was not the most favorable ground for defense, but it effectively covered the South Side Railroad just two and a half miles to the north. Pickett would have much preferred to establish his position about a mile and a quarter farther back, behind Hatcher's Run, both because it placed a natural obstacle between himself and Sheridan, and because it was closer to the Confederate lines. But as a dutiful subordinate he was forced to make his stand at Five Forks. If indeed Lee chose the position, drawing a line in the mud and ordering Pickett to hold it, then he bears a large share of the blame for what happened next.

Not liking either his orders or the ground he was to hold, Pickett sulked for the next twenty-four hours, refusing to communicate with headquarters. During that time the fate of the army and of the entire Confederate cause was sealed. By midmorning of April 1, Pickett had his troops dug in around Five Forks, with his wagons safely across Hatcher's Run under the watchful eye of Tom Rosser's cavalry. Expecting reinforcements and perhaps even a diversionary attack from Dick Anderson's sector of the lines, he did not demand the strongest possible entrenchments from his men. He was also confident that Sheridan would halt and regroup after the previous day's heavy fighting. He was so confident that in the early afternoon he rode off to Tom Rosser's camp, some two miles behind his lines, to partake of a lunch of freshly caught shad, compliments of Rosser. He was joined by his senior cavalry commander and fellow *bon vivant* Fitzhugh Lee. Neither Pickett nor Lee notified their next-in-command where they were going, and the "shad bake" turned into a convivial three-hour affair. During their absence, Sheridan's cavalry, reinforced now by Warren's 16,000 infantry, struck the ill-prepared Confederate lines and caved them in, capturing more than 5,000 men, eleven regimental flags and four artillery pieces. In less than an hour, the entire position was overrun, and those who were not killed or captured were sent fleeing for their lives. To his credit, Pickett attempted to get back to his lines in order to organize a defense, but his actions were too little and too late.

Library of Congress, Washington, D.C.

"Sheridan's Charge at Five Forks, Virginia, April 1, 1865." Lithograph from a painting by A. G. Redwood.

Then Pickett compounded his error by failing to send immediate word to Lee of what had happened. Instead, he disappeared in the panic-stricken flight of his command. He would remain out of touch for a remarkable twenty-four hours, during which time Lee remained virtually in the dark.[6] Later, when Pickett had time to reflect on this latest disaster to befall him, he put the blame on Lee: first, for ordering him to hold such a poor position as Five Forks; and second, for failing to send the reinforcements and launch the diversion he had requested. Unfortunately for this argument, no communique from Lee containing the fateful "Hold!" directive has ever turned up in official papers, although Pickett's adjutant, Walter Harrison, later insisted it was sent.[7]

As passed on by LaSalle Pickett and Walter Harrison, Pickett's memories of what transpired at Five Forks and who bore responsibility for the debacle were quite different from Lee's.

The former's feelings at the time were probably more in line with those of Gouverneur K. Warren, who told Philip Sheridan just before the battle, "Bobby Lee is always getting people into trouble."[8]

Lee's first premonition that his lines had been broken came in the form of incomplete reports from his nephew Fitzhugh and an unnamed Confederate captain who arrived at his headquarters at Trumball House after nightfall on April 1. Neither report revealed the true scope of the disaster, which only became apparent around 4:00 a.m., April 2, when Charles Venable of Lee's staff happened to be standing in the yard as Confederate wagons from Rosser's campsite came tearing by at breakneck speed, the drivers shouting that Yankees were right behind them. Lee and his staff, plus Generals Longstreet and A.P. Hill were all at Turnbull House at the time and would come close to being captured.

During that same night of April 1-2, Lee had already sent a dispatch to Secretary of War John C. Breckenridge outlining what he knew of the situation, which was not much. The one person who could have furnished a clear picture of things on the Confederate right was still incommunicado. As Lee admitted to Breckenridge, "General Pickett's present position is not known."[9] Pickett had not reported in since around 2:00 a.m. on the night of March 31-April 1. Under the circumstances, such silence was so extraordinary that Lee might have been excused for assuming that Pickett was either dead or captured.

By noon of April 2, Lee at last had his first clear picture of the disaster that had befallen his army. He telegraphed Breckenridge that he would try to hold his current position until nightfall, then withdraw north of the Appomattox and concentrate his remaining forces near the Danville Railroad.[10] He got his army stumbling westward that night, but his communications with Richmond had been cut, and he had little idea where he was going. As a result of this pell-mell flight, 350,000 rations for the army were left sitting on a railroad siding in Richmond because the Confederate quartermaster did not know where to send them. They were destroyed by official order when the capital was evacuated.[11]

This entire string of disasters—the loss of Five Forks, the breaking of the Petersburg lines, the destruction of essential rations, and the fall of Richmond—could all be traced directly back to George Pickett's bad judgment and failure of will. By halting his successful attack on Sheridan he allowed the latter to regroup and launch a ferocious counter-attack. By failing to anticipate and prepare for such an attack he had allowed Grant to achieve the breakthrough he had been seeking for ten months. This explains why the infamous "shad bake" has always been considered such a black mark on George Pickett's record. Lee may indeed have recalled his cautionary words to Jefferson Davis the previous August: "To succeed it is necessary to set the example, and this necessarily confines [officers] to their duties, their camp and mess, which is disagreeable *and deprives them of pleasant visits and dinners.*" [emphasis added][12] Even Lee could not have imagined what disastrous consequences this one "pleasant dinner" would have.

Fortunately for Pickett, Lee did not know of the infamous shad bake at the time, and it is highly doubtful that he ever learned of it. The story did not even come out until 1880 when Tom Rosser testified at Gouverneur K. Warren's court of inquiry regarding his part in the Battle of Five Forks, and by that time Lee had been dead for ten years.[13] Whatever anger Lee felt toward Pickett as a result of Five Forks, it was based on Pickett's lack of vigilance at his assigned post, not his presence that day at a fish feast, which was probably to Pickett's benefit because food was another indulgence that Lee did not allow himself. As Jefferson Davis once noted, "his fare in camp was [always] of the simplest."[14]

Even without factoring in the shad bake, Five Forks may have been the point at which Lee finally gave up on George Pickett, although he did not take action immediately. Other officers had taken note of the fact that, "Lee was sometimes too lenient with the failures of his generals, even when their delinquencies bore disastrous consequences."[15] But even Lee had his limits. Two of Pickett's contemporaries, men who served in his command, firmly believed that the commanding general intended nothing less than court martial and dismissal for contribution to the disaster at Five Forks. Randolph H. McKim, aide-de-camp to Brigadier General George H. Steuart, had "no doubt that he [Pickett] was relieved of his command after the battle." And fellow shad-baker Tom Rosser wrote in the Philadelphia *Weekly Times* in 1885 that, "Pickett's conduct at Five Forks was the cause of Lee's losing all confidence in him and had the opportunity been given he would have been court-martialed." These opinions, being published and therefore widely disseminated, are most likely the origin for the subsequent story that Lee either ordered Pickett's arrest or was on the verge of doing so when the end came at Appomattox. For Rosser it was a simple matter: Pickett had "failed to guard his left flank, and he failed to rejoin his command" when he received word that the enemy was advancing.[16] While Rosser was not speaking for Lee, these could well have been the precise points on which Lee based his own judgment.

The popular view of Five Forks as the breaking point in the relationship between Lee and Pickett has continued down to the present day. Two of the foremost modern authorities on Lee have stated that "but for the complete collapse which followed so soon on the disaster at Five Forks, the commander at Five Forks would probably have been called to account for it."[17] The fact was, there was no time for courts-martial or courts of inquiry at this point, and the army needed every man and officer it could get just to survive. Lee had an army to save. By the time Longstreet saw him some twelve hours after the battle, the commanding general was able to speak of Pickett's great defeat without bitterness, which is not to say he had forgotten it.[18]

It might have been better for George Pickett had he stayed lost after Five Forks, but he rejoined the army somewhere on the retreat toward Appomattox, in time to play a major part in one final disaster before the curtain came down. On April 6, Union cavalry swooped down on the rear of the Confederate army and routed General Richard Ewell's rear guard at Sayler's Creek. In the process they smashed what was left of Dick Anderson's corps, capturing nearly 8,000 men and destroying most of the Confederate wagon train. Among the officer captives was none other than Lee's eldest son Custis, whose exact fate that day was unknown to his father because of the chaotic conditions on the field. Pickett's command, attached to Anderson's Corps, was one of the first to break, and Pickett with members of his staff fled the field on horseback leaving the men to their fate.[19] Anderson was also among the first to leave the field in another disgraceful display of leadership. He and Pickett dropped out of sight for the next two days, but they were not forgotten. General Henry Wise complained to Lee after the battle that Pickett's disorganized command in their headlong flight had "interfered" with his own men, still trying to maintain a defensive front at the time.[20]

Lee vented his initial wrath on Bushrod Johnson, who reported to him just after the battle. He had nothing to say about Pickett or Anderson, but he must have been struck by the bitter assessment of General Wise, who observed, "It's not the men who're deserting the ranks, but the officers who are deserting the men who're disorganizing your army."[21] Pickett, Johnson, and Anderson were simply the most prominent culprits in that sweeping indictment. Indeed, Pickett's unequaled string of controversial performances to date had made him the "Peck's Bad Boy" of the Army of Northern Virginia. And he did not help his case by speaking out against Lee publicly. It was widely reported that he "abused and criticized" the commanding general for not surrendering the pitiful remnants of the army days before Appomattox.[22] George Pickett, for one, would not go "quietly into the darkness."

8 Dismissed From the Army

Lee's official response came two days after Sayler's Creek on April 8, and when he finally acted, the axe fell on all three disgraced officers. Lee issued orders for their dismissal from the army. The move was not unexpected, and the orders may not have been entirely punitive. He had stated just the day before in the presence of General William Mahone, "I give notice of my purpose to [diminish] the number of Corps and division commanders in this army."[1] Still, such an uncharacteristically harsh action raises a multitude of questions about everything from the timing and wording of the orders to the reactions of the three cashiered officers. None of these questions has a ready answer because the official orders have been lost to history, and not one of the principals ever commented on the matter afterwards. According to General Eppa Hunton, who was one of Pickett's brigadiers until captured at Sayler's Creek, Pickett was not just dismissed by Lee, but was ordered to report to President Davis "wherever he could find him."[2] If true, such humiliation goes beyond the punishment imposed on Anderson and Johnson, implying that Pickett was not just relieved of command but placed under arrest. Hunton does not elaborate. But the fact remains that Lee did not want Pickett with the army any longer.

It was Lee's normal practice to juggle subordinates rather than resort to outright dismissal. But these were not normal times. Just a week earlier, Lee had sent General Jubal Early home after the latter had ground down the Army of the Valley in a series of battles trying to stop Sheridan in the Shenandoah. "Your reverses in the Valley, of which the public and the army judge chiefly by the results, have, I fear, impaired your influence, both with the people and the soldiers," Lee explained in a letter to the dejected Early.[3]

Now it was Pickett's (and Johnson's and Anderson's) turn. For only the second time in his three-year tenure with the Army of Northern Virginia, Lee dismissed one of his officers. However shocking they may have been, Lee's orders, at least to Pickett, were not widely known throughout the army at the time. Eppa Hunton did not find out about Pickett's dismissal until twenty-five years after the fact, and General Fitzhugh Lee refused to believe it until Walter Taylor assured him in writing that it was true in 1903.[4]

By keeping a lid on the affair, Lee not only kept most of his own officers in the dark, but historians as well. The result was a lot of speculation later on that did little to clear up the mystery. Was Pickett cashiered for Five Forks? For Sayler's Creek? For being a malcontent on the retreat? Or for all three? Except for Pickett and Lee, few were in a position to know. One of those who was privileged to know the truth was Walter Taylor, Lee's adjutant-general whose duty it was to write out the commanding general's orders. He said years later that Lee had told him at the time the "reason" for the dismissal, but Taylor, exhibiting the same protectiveness toward Lee that all of Marse Robert's staff did, refused to divulge it.[5]

Unlike what happened with "Old Jube," there is no indication that Lee felt obliged to reassure Pickett that "my confidence in your ability, zeal and devotion to the cause is unimpaired," nor, again unlike Early, did the recipient take care to preserve Lee's words for posterity. The orders to Pickett were either thrown away or carelessly laid aside. We can only surmise, on the basis of Lee's letter to Early, that the commanding general was forthright about the reasons for his action, without trying to make excuses or trying to coat the bitter pill.

The entire affair is made all the more puzzling by an encounter between Lee and Pickett the next day, April 9, the date of the surrender at Appomattox. According to reliable sources, Lee remarked upon seeing Pickett, "I thought that man was no longer with this Army."[6] No one today can say for sure in what spirit Lee intended the remark; he could have been expressing contempt, astonishment, or bemusement. Charles Venable told John Mosby it was said with "deep feeling," and the historical consensus today leans toward contempt as the most likely.[7] In any event, Lee could not have been too dismayed by seeing his troublesome lieutenant still hanging around because the very next day, April 10, he sent a communique to Pickett requesting an official report on the activities of his command since the breakout from Petersburg.[8]

Pickett apparently did not consider himself dismissed because two days after the surrender he was still signing paroles, "Maj. Genl. Comdg." Nor did Pickett's adjutant, Colonel Walter Harrison, believe that his boss had been cashiered. The man who subsequently became the official historian of Pickett's Division called the argument that Pickett and the others had been relieved of command just before the surrender an "absurd rumor."[9]

Adding further mystery to the sequence of events—disgrace, dismissal, chance encounter—is the persistent story in later years that Pickett never received the orders relieving him of command and ordering him to Davis. Such a claim is rebutted by the clear recollection of Colonel Venable that he personally delivered the orders to Pickett on April 8, but Venable was not questioned about it until years later. Possibly, a slip-up occurred at Lee's headquarters under the chaotic conditions at the end which might have caused his orders to be misplaced or misdirected. If the orders were not delivered, Pickett had every right to be with the army on April 9; if they were, he was in open defiance of his commanding general, an offense in any army and sufficient reason for astonishment on Lee's part when he saw him the next day.

There is also the awkward matter of due process. Whatever orders Lee issued dismissing Pickett and the others from the Army of Northern Virginia, they did not conform to the procedure established by the Confederate Congress in October, 1862.[10] By law, an "examining board" should have been convened to consider the matter prior to any action the commanding general might take. Lee's recommendation undoubtedly would have been rubber-stamped by his superiors in Richmond, but even the appearance of due process was not followed here. In bypassing due process, was Lee in a hurry to put a distasteful job behind him, or was this a matter of extraordinary circumstances dictating extraordinary measures? As chaotic as things were on the retreat from the Petersburg lines, no one could realistically have expected Lee to take time out and convene an examining board.

The exact nature of the official relationship between Lee and Pickett when the final curtain came down at Appomattox is unclear enough to provide grist for all sorts of speculations and explanations. Both Lee and Pickett defenders put the best possible face on it. Neither a vindictive Lee nor a defiant Pickett serve as a constructive addition to the myth of the Lost Cause.

If we accept the conventional wisdom that Lee did indeed dismiss Pickett from the army (along with Dick Anderson and Bushrod Johnson) right before the curtain came down, the motivation behind the orders is the most mysterious part of the affair. Lee's respectful biographer, Douglas Southall Freeman, takes great pains to justify the commanding general's decision as a practical matter, not some sort of vindictive punishment inflicted on an unfortunate officer "in the hour of defeat." Freeman argues that the assignment of Pickett's and Johnson's troops, of Anderson's Corps, to the corps of John Gordon made all three officers—Pickett, Anderson and Johnson—"supernumerary," *i.e.*, without commands befitting their ranks. This meant in simple terms that without any troops, Pickett and Johnson had no divisions, and without the troops of their divisions, Anderson had no corps. And they could hardly be reassigned replacing others who had "done their duty." Therefore, to retain them in the field with no role in the army's future operations would inflict unnecessary "humiliation" on them.[11] This interpretation echoes the statement by William Mahone that Lee had already decided on April 5 to carry out a consolidation of the army's officer corps.

This argument is not entirely convincing, however. It ignores the fact that other high-ranking officers, most notably Isaac Trimble at Gettysburg, had accompanied the army on previous campaigns without the benefit of official command, yet with Lee's implicit approval, while awaiting assignment as needed. The history of the Confederate army also records the names of other officers who at various times attached themselves without appointment to fighting commands, *e.g.*, W.H.C. Whiting at Fort Fisher in January 1865. In other words, there was plenty of precedent for unassigned officers to "volunteer" their services in an army desperately short of manpower.

The supernumerary argument also ignores the fact that there were brigadiers in the army, some of whom had joined the flight at Sayler's Creek, leading company-sized units at the end. Indeed, at the end, not a single officer in the Army of Northern Virginia was leading a full-strength unit. And while Pickett's Division was far from full-strength, it was hardly annihilated. There were still 1,031 men present on the rolls when it surrendered on April 9, 1865, more than enough men to justify retention intact with its commanding officer had Lee been so inclined.[12]

If Lee's motivation for dismissing Pickett was the latter's dereliction of duty, as John Mosby maintained, then the proximate cause had to be what happened at Five Forks and/or Sayler's Creek. Lee had no use for officers who were not where they were supposed to be. Benjamin Huger discovered this in June 1862, when he was absent from his headquarters during an attack on his outposts and Lee sent him orders to take his proper place with his troops "and to remain with them."[13] Soon thereafter Huger was relieved of active command and relegated to inspection duties. Pickett's strange absence from his lines when the Federals struck at Five Forks, then six days later his flight from the field at Sayler's Creek, were both sufficient cause to draw the wrath of the commanding general.

But even this entirely reasonable explanation raises some troubling questions. If Pickett were being punished for Five Forks, then why did the ever fair and honorable Lee not take action against his nephew Fitzhugh Lee for that officer's disreputable part in the same battle? After all, Fitzhugh was Pickett's lunch companion at the infamous shad bake when Sheridan caught the Confederates off-guard. And if Robert E. Lee's action was, in part or in whole, punishment for Pickett's ignoble flight at Sayler's Creek, why did the commanding general wait two days to respond, by which time the gesture had lost any exemplary meaning?

At least part of the answer comes from a closer examination of Lee's character. This mild-mannered man contained within him a contradiction that has gone largely unnoticed until his latest biographer took up the pen. That contradiction, as noted by Professor Emory Thomas, was that while Lee could be aggressive to the point of foolhardiness in battle, he instinctively shrank from personal confrontation in all other situations.[14] He preferred to let his actions speak for themselves, and relied on vague instructions or mild sarcasm to convey his intentions to others. It is not difficult at all to imagine Lee agonizing for five days over whether or not to dismiss three of his most senior officers from the army in April 1865. Time and again Lee demonstrated that he did not like to exercise his considerable authority with a heavy hand. This same trait also explains why it has always been so difficult for some to imagine that he would issue such orders at all. But a careful consideration of the circumstantial evidence does lead to the conclusion that Lee intended to send George Pickett home before the surrender at Appomattox.

9 When Johnny (and George and Robert) Come Marching Home Again

The dismissal order, the flurry of angry correspondence after Gettysburg, and the fiascoes at New Berne, Five Forks, and Sayler's Creek were all part of the bigger puzzle of the Lee-Pickett relationship. Speculation would persist even if the story ended here and the two men had never crossed paths again after the war. But according to LaSalle, the Lee and Pickett families remained on good terms even after the events of Appomattox. Mrs. Pickett, both an extension of and alter ego for her husband in the postwar years, was probably speaking for George and herself when she called General Lee "dignified, warm-hearted and impartial." She also described him as a man who "paid no more attention to personal antagonisms than to personal affection in the management of the army," which should certainly have worked in her husband's favor.[1] She once wrote graciously of her husband's nemesis, "About the only thing I ever resented in General Lee was that he always called me 'Sweet Nansemond,'" thus either forgetting his wartime clashes with her husband or else choosing not to speak of them publicly.[2]

Years later LaSalle wrote loving biographical sketches of both General and Mrs. Lee which did much to dispel any suggestions of a rupture between the two men. Far from estrangement in fact, she posited a long-running personal friendship, complete with house visits and sentimental gestures, which endured war and Reconstruction. Mrs. Pickett never said how or when this friendship began, and it certainly did not exist before the Civil War. It is hard to imagine such a friendship developing during the war either, due to the vast gulf that separated their respective positions in the Confederate army command and on duty and sacrifice.

LaSalle does not stop with the men's relationship. In her version of things, the two general's wives, Mrs. Pickett and Mrs. Lee, got along famously, perhaps because they were not subject to the burdens of command and army politics. In one conversation recalled by LaSalle, Mary Custis Lee said, "I know the General always does his best and am content to be quiet when he wins and calm when he loses."[3] Although Mrs. Lee said it, the remark might just as easily have come from LaSalle.

The verified clashes between Lee and Pickett during the war are a more accurate reflection of their true relationship than the tender moments described by LaSalle in her beguiling reminiscences. But details aside, her reminiscences at least suggest that there was never a complete break between the two men. Mrs. Pickett had vivid recollections of "Marse Robert's" personal visits to the Pickett household in the years immediately following the war. When the Picketts' son Corbell was suffering from a fatal illness in 1867, Lee came to visit the boy and sat by his bed trying to comfort him. Shortly before Corbell died, Lee was present at the bedside, kneeling to say a humble prayer for the little boy. This touching tableau, as depicted by LaSalle, was her "last sweet memory of General Lee, for I never saw him again."[4]

But her husband did, and the meeting produced the usual sparks that always seemed to follow whenever the two men got together. Toward the end of March 1870, a sick and dying Lee visited Richmond for the last time, at least partly to consult physicians about his deteriorating heart condition. He was told he did not have long to live.[5] His daughter Agnes traveled with him, and they stayed for three days, lodging in the Exchange Hotel, a stately, five-story, antebellum building on Franklin Street favored by Lee during his visits to the city. During their stay, Lee did not venture far from his room due to the state of his health, but that did not prevent old friends and comrades from flocking to see him. Everyone in Richmond, it seemed, wanted to express their love and admiration for the old gentleman. He held court in one of the hotel parlors, which is where he was the day he and George Pickett met.

Pearce Civil War Collection, Navarro College, Corsicana, TX.

Heretofore unpublished Matthew Brady photograph of Robert E. Lee during his last eighteen months of life. Taken at the photographer's Washington, D.C. studio. According to lore, Lee was pressured by the photographer to sit for this picture during a brief visit to the capital on business in 1869.

At this time Pickett was maintaining a residence at the more modest Ballard House, also on Franklin Street, for conducting business when he was in Richmond, which was quite often. The Ballard was connected to the Exchange by an iron bridge above the street, which led many to regard them as practically one sprawling hotel. It was almost inevitable that the two men would meet. Among the steady stream of admirers who came to pay their respects was Colonel John S. Mosby, the former "Gray Ghost," still wiry and youthful looking at the age of thirty-six. Lee had considered Mosby one of his most valuable lieutenants during the war for the always accurate intelligence he provided. After Appomattox Mosby had resumed his pre-war law practice in Virginia and became one of the first to make his peace with the hated Yankees. The brash and romantic-minded Mosby was an outspoken individualist who also happened to have a puckish sense of humor. The fact that he was also a name-dropper and a gossip-monger just made him that much more interesting to know. Nonetheless, it was a volatile combination of traits which regularly got him into trouble.

At the end of March 1870, however, he was just another one of Lee's erstwhile officers who wished to pay his respects to the beloved commander. After his own audience with Lee ended he ran into Pickett who expressed an impulsive desire to likewise pay his respects one last time to the Great Man. Up to that moment the two men had managed to avoid each other.

It is doubtful if Pickett had actually had a one-on-one meeting with Lee since Appomattox, much less sat down and talked. They had never been close personal friends, contrary to the pleasant picture painted by LaSalle. Their post-war careers had taken them in opposite directions, though fate seemed determined to throw them together one way or another: After the close of the war, while under parole, both men were indicted on a charge of treason, Lee primarily as commander of the Army of Northern Virginia, Pickett because of a mass hanging of Unionists he had authorized at Kinston, North Carolina, in 1864. Pickett's response to being branded a traitor and outlaw was to pack up his family and flee to Canada where he remained until assured all charges would be dropped. For his part, Lee rode out the storm at home in Richmond, making himself available to all comers while scrupulously observing the terms of his parole. He remained very much a public man, however, sitting for an interview with the New York *Herald* only days after his return, and even agreeing to pose for famed photographer Matthew Brady to make a "historical picture".[6]

With their legal problems solved, Lee and Pickett proceeded to rebuild their lives from scratch. Robert E. Lee became a symbol of reunion and reconstruction, turning his back on his military career and championing higher education as the president of tiny Washington College. "Virginia wants all their aid, and all their support, and the presence of all her sons," he declared to those who contemplated flight or continued resistance. He also refused to cash in on his name and reputation to secure a comfortable living, though at least one shrewd Northern insurance company wanted to pay him to use his name on its letterhead, thereby helping to sell policies in the South.[7]

Pickett too had been faced with hard decisions after the war. Out of the army for the first time in twenty-three years, he fell on hard times that his years of duty had not equipped him to handle. But he also faced some problems that Lee did not. Not only did he bear the onus of being a "traitor," but like John Mosby who had a price placed on his head by General Grant, he was accused of being a war criminal. In the sorting out of the guilty and innocent in the public mind, this was something much more serious.[8] Pickett had good cause to fear for both his life and his freedom at the hands of a vindictively inclined Federal government. Even after that threat was removed with Andrew

Johnson's "Christmas Pardon" in 1868 granting full and unconditional amnesty to practically all Confederates, he had difficulty putting his life back together again. Part of the problem was that he had no practical skills except for his military training. By 1870 he had failed at farming and was selling life insurance to support his wife and only surviving son. In making calls on former comrades-in-arms, he found that the door was never closed to "General Pickett."

On the day in 1870 when Pickett went to see General Lee—either March 25, 26, or 27—Pickett made the decision to seek an interview with his former commanding general purely on whim, with perhaps a touch of nostalgia mixed in. It was a major mistake. Mosby described what followed as a "cold and formal interview" between the elderly commanding general and his troublesome lieutenant. Both men were so miserable and "embarrassed" by the reunion that Mosby thought it best to execute a strategic retreat. He ushered Pickett out of the room as soon as possible, but the denouement of the story did not occur until the two men were alone in the hall. Then and only then did Pickett reveal his true feelings, lashing out at Lee with a pent-up fury that surprised Mosby. "That old man...had my division slaughtered at Gettysburg," raged Pickett.

"Well," Mosby replied wryly, "it made you immortal." But later after reflecting further on the remark, he decided that Pickett had given "the wrong reason for his unfriendly feelings."[9]

The real reason, Mosby decided, was that Lee had placed Pickett under arrest just days before Appomattox. This bit of startling information— and it was startling because Lee had never been known to place any general officer under arrest during four years of war—came from Charles Venable, the former staff officer, in an 1892 conversation between Mosby and Venable. Venable did not give any reason so Mosby supplied his own: "I suppose [it was] for the Five Forks affair."[10] Venable's statement, if Mosby heard him correctly, was patently untrue, as another member of Lee's staff stated publicly when Mosby's story came out. Walter Taylor was closer to Robert E. Lee than any other officer on the staff, and his word can be taken as gospel when he "denied emphatically" that General Lee ever placed Pickett under arrest.[11]

Taylor, Venable, and Mosby were scarcely more than acquaintances of Pickett, so they had no way of knowing his real feelings, or the anger he had carried around bottled up inside for nearly seven years. Only LaSalle and perhaps James Longstreet knew the truth. Ever since Gettysburg, Pickett felt that he had been denied the right to tell his side of the events of July 3, 1863, by orders of Robert E. Lee. In the process he had also been denied the right to vent his anger and sense of betrayal. Ever since Lee had returned his battle report, he had considered himself sworn to secrecy.[12] He carried that self-imposed obligation of silence with him to his grave, and after he died it was taken up by LaSalle Pickett. Over the years the burden of that silence had gotten heavier and heavier, as he watched Lee being enshrined by a defeated people. The South had forgiven Lee for Gettysburg, but George Pickett never could.

After being papered over for more than four decades, the estrangement between Lee and Pickett burst upon the public in 1911 when John S. Mosby wrote his "Personal Recollections of General Lee" for *Munsey's Magazine*. It is only fitting that Mosby be the one to break the story since the former "Gray Ghost" always enjoyed "stirring the pot" where his esteemed compatriots were concerned. Still, the revelation exposed a major fissure in the Lost Cause mythology and could not have been much more shocking if Mosby had revealed that Lee was a pre-war abolitionist.

For the first time, most people learned that all had not been peace and harmony between Robert E. Lee and one of his most famous lieutenants. The *Munsey's* piece was picked up almost before it hit the streets by the Richmond *Times-Dispatch* which habitually functioned in the role of official organ for Defenders of the Lost Cause. It printed the juiciest parts from "Personal Recollections of General Lee" in its Tuesday, March 21 issue. The response was electric: Numerous readers angrily wrote in to deny the article and damn the author. The newspaper published the responses from two of the most adamant and informed letter-writers. Miss K.C. Stiles of Richmond stated that she had been present in the Ballard House parlor on the morning of the notorious meeting between Lee and Pickett. Also present, she recalled, were Mosby, Lee's daughter Agnes, and sitting nearby, "twenty or more tourists listening and gazing at General Lee." Miss Stiles insisted, "I did not see the stiffness that Colonel Mosby spoke of." Instead, "We chatted together a while, and then those gentlemen took leave."[13]

Here was an eye-witness supposedly repudiating everything Mosby had said. But her version had the appearance of a white-wash, first because by her own admission she was not present in Lee's room when, out of the public eye, the men would have felt free to let their true emotions show; and second, because she felt obliged to remind Mosby of Lee's place in history. "Colonel Mosby should know by now that the military courts of the world some years ago announced that the greatest captain of the nineteenth century was General Robert E. Lee.... So that his place in history is assured." This was not an objective observer, nor someone who had known Lee or Pickett as long and as intimately as John Mosby.

The other reader selected by the newspaper to answer Mosby was Dr. M. G. Elzey, former surgeon of Eppa Hunton's brigade and "General Pickett's personal medical advisor." Elzey had been at Pickett's side in those final days before Appomattox. The doctor stated emphatically that Lee had never placed Pickett under arrest, which was a point he should have taken up with Charles Venable since Mosby only claimed in "Personal Recollections of General Lee" to be reporting what Venable had told him. More to the point, Elzey "positively affirmed as a matter within my personal knowledge" that "no interruption of personal relationship between the two men ever took place." On the contrary, Pickett after the war spoke of General Lee "always in terms of the highest veneration and respect."[14]

But Elzey was taking aim at a straw man, *viz.*, the unfounded charge that Lee placed Pickett under arrest, rather than the true state of affairs. And his letter also smacked of Lost Cause dogma when he added, "All right-minded men must deplore the disposition to attack and disparage his former associates in arms in our lost, righteous cause." Any suggestion that Lee and one of his lieutenants might have been on the outs was a blow not just at the sainted Lee but at the Lost Cause itself. The doctor concluded by questioning Mosby's *bona fides*, pointing out that the old colonel had first deserted the Democratic party to declare himself a Republican, then "sought and obtained" Federal office. Therefore, syllogistically, Mosby's version of history was specious because Mosby himself was a turncoat! Yet the preponderance of testimony from other veterans was on Mosby's side, at least insofar as the bad feelings between Lee and Pickett were concerned, and all the Lost Cause champions to the contrary could not change that.

Mosby's revelations became a permanent part of Civil War historiography with the publication of his *Memoirs* in 1917, but the damage had already been done by then. He definitely struck a nerve, in the process proving two things: that Lee's defenders were still numerous and passionate, and that Mosby's memory was faulty. What apparently happened is that Mosby confused Lee's dismissal orders to Pickett, Anderson, and Johnson, with arrest orders, and then provided his own reason for the latter. Venable probably did deliver special orders to Pickett, but they were not arrest orders because the man who wrote them out, Lieutenant Colonel Walter Taylor adamantly denied any such thing.

But the tempest in a teapot stirred up by Mosby's revelations only distracts attention from the very real problems between Lee and Pickett. The 1870 Richmond hotel encounter was only the postscript to a relationship that had begun and ended years earlier. Pickett's outburst against Lee, more than any other piece of evidence, indicates how deeply and virulently the bad feelings ran between the two men even five years after the war. Lee left no clue as to his own feelings on that occasion, but it is obvious from Mosby's description that the elderly gentleman was uncomfortable with the meeting and made no attempt to put Pickett at ease or to extend the hand of friendship.

There would be no second chance. Seven months later Lee died in Lexington, after a lingering illness, on October 12, 1870. The funeral was a rather stark affair, as he desired, attended by his college family and close relatives. Seasonal rains kept most outsiders away, but this did not prevent a "universal sense of sorrow" on both sides of the Mason-Dixon line as the news was carried by telegraph wire and newspaper across the country. In Lexington, Richmond, and other Southern cities, businesses closed, windows were draped in black crepe, and flags were flown at half mast. Across the state, bells tolled out the sad news, reminding every citizen within hearing range how much Virginia loved Marse Robert. Veterans of the Army of Northern Virginia gathered in somber groups to reminisce about following him without question through four years of war and perhaps to recall small moments when he might have spoken to one of them personally. The whole state was in deep mourning. Everyone had loved Marse Robert, or so it seemed.

Two days after his death on Wednesday, memorial services were held in Lexington, then the remains lay in state in the Washington College chapel until interment on Sunday. George Pickett was not in attendance to pay his last respects, not surprising in light of the quiet, modest way things were handled by the family. In the days that followed, Lee's former officers came forward to offer one testimonial after another in the newspapers. And George Pickett's voice was strangely missing from among all these heartfelt eulogies. It is hard to imagine that some scribe did not hunt him down for an appropriate quote when Charles Marshall, Jubal Early, John Imboden, William Preston Johnston, Isaac Trimble, John Gordon and numerous others all made public statements. This is particularly surprising since Pickett was living in Richmond at the time, and it would have been easy for a reporter to interview the man whose name was intrinsically linked with Lee's through Gettysburg.

Nor did Pickett join in when many of those same former officers and admirers formed the Lee Memorial Association just a week after Lee's death to raise money for a suitable statue to the Great Man. Virtually every other Virginia officer of Lee's former army signed on to the organization. It is not enough to say that Pickett was simply not a joiner; he had no problem joining the Confederate Veterans' group that organized in Richmond on November 4, 1870, just three weeks after Lee's death. George Pickett was one of the first officers elected by the "Society of the Army of Northern Virginia," soon to become the Confederate Veterans' Organization. He served as a vice president, alongside Edward Johnson, Dabney Maury, William Smith, and six other notables.[15]

Whatever his other faults, George Pickett was not one to nurture a grudge against someone beyond the grave, no matter how convinced he was of the righteousness of his feelings. Death brings closure to all feuds one way or another. But neither did he wish to join the chorus of hosannas and lamentations being offered for the "old man who had my division slaughtered at Gettysburg." In Pickett's defense, it must be stated that he continued to keep his deepest feelings of rancor to himself and avoid the urge to beat up on Lee in print after his nemesis was gone. Certainly he could have found a ready vehicle for his recriminations if he had so wished, in a publication such as the New York *Tribune*, which referred to Lee's "repeated blunders and failures" in an editorial occasioned by his death.[16] But Pickett preferred to do his venting in private, to his wife and perhaps his brother Charles. He never provided any juicy quotes to fuel the fires of debate.

Pickett died July 30, 1875, in Norfolk, Virginia, while on a business trip to that old seaport town. Never very healthy, some mysterious ailment sickened him, causing him to go to the local hospital. Though attended by both Norfolk and Richmond doctors, he never rallied and breathed his last with family gathered around him. Initially, he was given a quiet burial in Norfolk before being brought back to Richmond for final burial in Hollywood Cemetery. Even in death he received somewhat shabby treatment, his gravesite being covered up in later years by the Virginia Division monument so that today no headstone for the man himself exists. The town that had been home to the Picketts for two generations did not erect a monument in his memory, name any streets or public buildings after him, or in any way honor George Pickett as they did Robert E. Lee and other Confederate leaders. It was as if his break with Lee had also alienated him from his hometown and made him *persona non grata* in the pantheon of the Lost Cause. It would not be until years later that LaSalle Pickett, his adoring widow, would rehabilitate and rework his image in her speeches and writings, and indeed in her very person, to gain him a belated place in the band of Southern heroes with whom he had fought.

One is tempted to reach for literary parallels to help explain the relationship between Lee and Pickett. In Shakespeare's drama, *The Two Gentlemen of Verona*, the play begins as a virtual paean to love, then progresses through pain and sorrow enroute to a harmonious ending that concludes everything on a note of healing: "One feast, one house, one mutual happiness." Unfortunately, for these two gentlemen of Virginia, Robert E. Lee and George E. Pickett, there could be no such happy ending to their story. They were never able to peacefully resolve their differences or to find common ground, even years after the war that had divided them ended. They carried their hard feelings to the grave, leaving others to sweep the whole thing under the carpet when they were gone.

As the image of Robert E. Lee the "Marble Man" was carefully constructed in the post-war years and incorporated into the larger Myth of the Lost Cause, anything that did not fit the offi-

Author's collection.

The stirring Lee Monument on Seminary Ridge at Gettysburg, looking out over the field of Pickett's Charge for all eternity. Ironically, the nominal leader of Pickett's Charge has no monument in his honor anywhere on the field, although a tablet to one of his brigadiers, Lewis Armistead, is at the high-water mark on Cemetery Ridge.

cial version was played down or dismissed out of hand. John Mosby was the first to break publicly with the official version, but many others had detected first-hand the strong feelings of animosity between Lee and Pickett. Years after the fact, the story was told among Richmond old-timers, unverifiable at this late date, that Pickett had gone so far as to stand under Lee's hotel window and shout insults up at the old man. While Pickett certainly had the motive and the opportunity during Lee's last visit to Richmond, it is hard to put much faith in such an incredible story that lacks specific attribution. Still, the fact that the story has persisted and even achieved a level of acceptance in local lore over the years shows the public's willingness to believe that a deep rift existed between Lee and Pickett, whatever its origins. It is hard to imagine the same sort of story even being told about Lee and any of his other lieutenants.

It would be nice if each man's version of events, in his own words, could be evaluated, but neither Lee nor Pickett proved to be a memoirist. Immediately after the war Lee seriously considered writing a history of the Army of Northern Virginia that would be "a tribute...to the worth of its noble officers and soldiers." He even went so far as to begin gathering material from his scattered lieutenants, but he abandoned the project quickly, deciding instead to maintain an Olympian silence to the end.[17]

During his lifetime, Pickett never had any literary aspirations. He reportedly kept a wartime diary, but if so, that, like his legendary "Gettysburg Report" has long since been lost to history. His only known writing consisted of a steady stream of love letters intended for the eyes of LaSalle only.

Other veterans of the Army of Northern Virginia, however, were not so reticent, and proved more than willing to take up the pen for their favorite hero or preferred version of events. A veritable host of authors, including Generals Jubal Early and William Jones, nephew Fitzhugh Lee, staff officer Walter Taylor, and British Field Marshall Viscount Wolseley, all wrote books which claimed to explain Lee's thinking at every turn. Pickett's able defenders were fewer but equally determined. They included Walter Harrison, James Longstreet, and the indefatigable LaSalle Pickett, all of whom perceived some sort of vague conspiracy against their champion. Yet none of the self-appointed apologists for either man was willing to honestly address the touchy subject of the Lee-Pickett feud.

Virginia Historical Society, Richmond, VA.

Detail from "The Four Seasons of the Confederacy: The Summer Mural," by French painter Charles Hoffbauer, depicting Lee and his officers at Gettysburg. Even in artistic imagination, George Pickett (second from right) is widely separated from his commanding general.

10 Why a Feud?

As a Virginian and a member of the Army of Northern Virginia, George Pickett stands virtually alone as the only one of "Lee's Lieutenants" whose image did not gain from his association with the South's greatest war hero. While others basked in his reflected glory, Pickett's career was completely eclipsed by the long shadow of Lee. One can leave it with the obvious fact that Robert E. Lee and George E. Pickett were as different as night and day and had an uneasy working relationship at best. But it is not that simple. Their differences seem to have been exacerbated by the situations into which they were constantly thrown. It seemed that disaster was never far off whenever those two were on the same field or involved in a common venture. Pickett could easily be dubbed "Lee's hard-luck general" because of his string of misfortunes during the war, but there is a connection between those misfortunes and Lee. Pickett might have fared better in his assignments with a change of scenery, like John Bankhead Magruder in 1862 when he was transferred from the Army of Northern Virginia to Texas where he became an instant hero. Serving under Joe Johnston late in the war might have worked wonders for George Pickett; it certainly did not hurt him early in the war before the Army of Northern Virginia became Lee's army.

Lee's attitude toward Pickett must be pieced together as much from what he did not say as from what he did say, from the dry language of official orders, and from his comparable reaction to other officers in similar circumstances. It is clear that Lee valued executive over administrative ability in his officers, while recognizing the value of both. A good executive officer could prepare men for battle and command them when battle came. A good administrative officer could juggle all the myriad details of independent command and accomplish his objective in the face of all obstacles. John Bankhead Magruder was not a particularly good executive officer, but he was a masterful administrator in the District of Texas, Trans-Mississippi Department. John Bell Hood was just the opposite: brilliant at leading men in battle but not particularly adept at administration. In George Pickett, Lee got neither. As executive officer of a division, Pickett was not attentive to details like drill and instruction, and as a department head, he was a timid, indecisive commander who shrank from taking initiative.

Lee's silence on Pickett is deafening. As more than one historian has pointed out, at one time or another Lee praised by name practically all of his lieutenant and major generals, although some, such as Wade Hampton, had to wait until after the war for their recognition.[1] George Pickett is the notable exception to this sweeping generalization. Although Lee commended Pickett's Division in glowing terms on more than one occasion, he never directly included General Pickett by name in those encomiums. Dick Anderson, John Bell Hood, Wade Hampton, Jubal Early, even D. H. Hill, Lee's most outspoken critic among his lieutenants—all came in for their share of praise—and this from the man who once said, "Where all [have done] so well, certainly it would be invidious and improper for me to particularize."[2] But particularize he did at one time or another in the case of virtually every senior officer save Pickett. The significance of this omission can be argued, but not the fact itself. One can search the record of Lee's wartime and postwar statements and nowhere does the name of George Pickett appear in condemnation, but nowhere is it singled out for praise either.

Lee had fond nicknames for several of his officers, the most notable being Jackson ("Stonewall"), Longstreet (his "old warhorse"), Jubal Early (his "bad old man"), A.P. Hill ("Little Powell"), and even Pickett's cousin Henry Heth ("Harry"). But no one ever heard Lee speak of George Pickett in any other way than as "General Pickett" or, once, as "that man," a dismissive term that calls to mind Lee's reference to the Federals as "those people." This whole name thing is nothing more than a bit of circumstantial evidence, but it adds another piece to the puzzle.

Lee's preferred method of handling fractious or dissatisfied subordinates was to finesse the problem rather than provoke direct confrontations. This method worked well with D.H. Hill,

James Longstreet, and Stonewall Jackson among others, allowing Lee to get the most out of them within the command structure of the Army of Northern Virginia. By comparison, even before their differences on the way home from Gettysburg, Lee seemed to have little use for George Pickett. Pickett's irrepressible romantic streak and his inattention to matters of drill and discipline in his command, as recorded in official correspondence, stand out as black marks against him in Lee's book. On more than one occasion he proved himself irresponsible and unreliable, and Lee's attitude about duty and responsibility were legendary in his own lifetime. "I cannot trust a man to control others who cannot control himself," was a guiding principle he followed in assembling his officer corps, as was a favorite piece of advice: "Do your duty in all things.... You cannot do more; you should never wish to do less."[3] Lee could tolerate errors in judgment, even bloody failure, as A.P. Hill learned after Bristoe Station, but not irresponsible behavior.[4]

We can only guess at all the factors that went into Lee's thinking. Since he had little occasion to directly observe Pickett, some of his information must have percolated up through the chain of command. The fact that Pickett aroused strong feelings of antipathy among some fellow officers probably colored the reports that Lee received and therefore influenced his impressions toward the negative. At the same time, friendship, fraternal ties, or Virginia roots might have been expected to give Pickett an inside track to promotions and better assignments, or at least gained him a little time to make a favorable impression. But Pickett could not even play those trump cards with any hope of success. The two men scarcely knew each other before the war, and the usual fraternal ties—Virginia, West Point, and the Old Army—applied equally to dozens of officers with whom Lee had no quarrel. The spiteful assertion of some officers like Lafayette McLaws that "Virginians [always] preferred Virginians" certainly does not fit Lee and Pickett.[5] Conversely, the short shrift which Pickett seems to have received from his commanding general cannot be chalked up to the sort of personal pique that poisoned so many working relationships in the Confederate army. To deny Pickett rank or responsibility on account of any personal animosity would have gone against everything we know about Lee. The unavoidable conclusion is that Lee's low opinion of Pickett was the result of Pickett's own actions.

To better understand the antipathy between Lee and Pickett, it is useful to return to the Lee-Jackson relationship. Lee's known fondness and admiration for Jackson went far beyond the latter's success on the battlefield, their similar offensive-mindedness, or even the fact that Jackson more than any other of Lee's lieutenants seemed able to read the commanding general's mind. Lee loved Jackson the man as much as he did Jackson the general. He identified with the reliable, self-sacrificing Stonewall who, even on his death bed, still thought of his men. As Jackson lay dying at Guiney's Station he was attended by his favorite chaplain who hovered at his bedside. Jackson sent him away with instructions to see to the men's spiritual needs first because, if he were to devote himself exclusively to Jackson, "it would be setting an example of self-gratification to the troops, [so] you had better stay at your post of duty. I have always tried to set the troops a good example."

Jackson had already given virtually the same instructions to his chief medical officer, Dr. Hunter McGuire, refusing, as McGuire told it, "to permit me to go with him...because complaints had been so frequently made of General officers, when wounded, carrying off with them the surgeons belonging to their commands." That would never be the case in Jackson's command, no matter how grievously wounded the lieutenant general might be.[6] Compared to this standard of selflessness, how much worse did Pickett's self-indulgent behavior look in leaving his command to take the trains into Richmond, making all-night rides to court LaSalle Corbell, or attending a shad bake behind the lines with the enemy in their front?

One more Lee story of relevance supports this conclusion. It tells how after Gettysburg he spoke highly of a certain officer's merits, saying that such worth deserved promotion. Several of his staff expressed surprise and reminded him that this particular officer had often talked disparagingly of the commanding general. "I cannot help that, he is a good soldier and would be useful in a higher position," Lee told them.[7] While the officer in question was not George Pickett, the point is apropos to Pickett. Had Pickett been a conscientious soldier and a hard fighter instead of just a troublesome lieutenant (*cf.* James Longstreet), there seems little doubt that his position in the Army of Northern Virginia would have been secure. He never was, and as a result he paid the price.

Because Gettysburg virtually defines the Lee-Pickett relationship, all discussion of that relationship eventually comes back to the events of July 3, 1863. The judgment of history is still out, but the judgment of Robert E. Lee seems quite clear. George Pickett was no coward, and there is no indication in the historical record that the man whose opinion mattered the most, General Lee, ever thought he was. Lee's displeasure with Pickett arose from other, complex causes. Lee, who as we have said, always believed that a division commander "fights his troops," questioned how well George Pickett had "fought" his division on the third day when so much evidence, not to mention rumor and innuendo, pointed to a complete abdication of his leadership responsibilities at a critical time in the action. That was a serious enough indictment, to be sure, which Pickett eventually paid for, but it was not cowardice. And Lee's dispatches of July 8 and 9 offer no ammunition to those who would brand Pickett a coward. To even suggest that Lee would have kept a man he considered a coward in the army is an insult to both George Pickett and Robert E. Lee.

We must look elsewhere for the causes of the rift between the two men. At least part of the problem that Pickett had with Lee seems to have been oedipal in nature. Lee was the classic stern, demanding, and distant father figure for all his soldiers who sought to please him even unto death. In Pickett's case, he longed more than most for a word of praise from the man they called "Marse Robert." That was all—simple acknowledgment on Lee's part that George Pickett was worthy. He wrote LaSalle after Pickett's Charge that some of his soldiers had expressed a willingness to do it again if Lee gave the word. "Isn't that reverential adoration, to be willing to be 'killed again' for a word of praise?" A little later, when the praise finally came from Lee, he exulted to LaSalle, "I've had the great gratification of receiving a most complimentary and explanatory note from General Lee." Even the fact that the praise was mostly for his men, not himself, did not dampen his exultation.[8]

For Lee's part, he may have seen in his troublesome subordinate reflections of his own father, the dissolute Lighthorse Harry Lee. The elder Lee squandered his family's resources, deserted them, disgraced the family name, and drank himself into an early grave. For the rest of his life, Lee had no use for hard-drinking, irresponsible men with weak characters. These feelings were more than the rational decisions of a good manager; they were deep-seated emotional responses to his own past. Lee was never able to completely resolve his feelings about his father, though he spent his adult life trying to do so by, among other things, paying visits to his grave in Georgia and editing a reissue of his memoirs. Lighthorse Harry Lee and long-haired George Pickett were not so very different, a fact that Lee was constantly reminded of during the war.

Another part of the explanation for the Lee-Pickett relationship is to be found in their differing mindsets. Lee functioned best in hierarchical relationships. He was comfortable with an arrangement where Jefferson Davis was his unquestioned superior while he himself was the superior of such able men as Jackson and Longstreet. Vertical relationships worked quite well for Lee and they explain his lifelong military success. He had his own concept of how an army operated. As he explained on more than one occasion, a brigadier "leads" his troops, a division commander "fights" his troops, a corps commander "commands," and a general of an army "directs."[9]

George Pickett, on the other hand, was only comfortable in lateral relationships. He resented authority and chafed at deferring to any man as his superior. He much preferred to consider himself an equal, but under wartime military conditions this was not a workable arrangement. For all their meeting of the minds with General Lee, Jackson and Longstreet always knew who the chief was. Pickett never understood his place in the hierarchy. He considered himself part of the cream of the Army of Northern Virginia, but without being willing to shoulder all the responsibilities and sacrifices that entailed. This sort of presumptuousness antagonized Lee to no end.[10]

Part of the problem on Lee's side might also be attributed to his deteriorating health as the war dragged on. The man who had been described by Winfield Scott during the Mexican War as "indefatigable" had become by the latter part of the Civil War a seriously ill, elderly man. He was afflicted by a combination of heart problems and intestinal ailments that sapped his strength and made him increasingly short-tempered. When he was feeling poorly, he was most "difficult," becoming sarcastic and intolerant. Numerous officers at one time or another felt his wrath, but no one tried his patience more than George Pickett.[11] After Gettysburg, perhaps if the war had gone better and he had felt fit, he would have been more tolerant of Pickett's failures. But by that time, Lee was no longer suffering fools gladly. As for Pickett, every sharply worded dispatch or exasperated reproof from his commanding general, instead of driving him to try harder, only made him more willful and withdrawn than ever.

The result was a star-crossed, even tragic relationship between these two professional soldiers and Virginia gentlemen. That a man of Pickett's sensitive and self-indulgent nature should blame his problems on Lee was totally in character. His bitter comment to Mosby in the Exchange Hotel provides strong evidence that Pickett believed Lee's hand was turned against him at least as early as Gettysburg. Pickett's festering resentment was not spontaneously born on that afternoon in 1870 when he and Mosby went calling.

That a man of Lee's deep and unswerving devotion to duty and honor should be offended by Pickett was also in character. Officers who were irresponsible, whether through drunkenness or incompetence or whatever, received only disdain from Lee. This was demonstrated when he "cleaned house" in the army after the Battle of Seven Pines, shuffling his senior officers to find a combination to his liking.

This is not to suggest that Lee ever attempted to derail Pickett's career, but he blocked it and held it back in subtle ways, albeit not without good reason. In all honesty, it is more accurate to say that Pickett derailed his own career, although he always enjoyed the benefit of powerful defenders both during and after the war, most notably James Longstreet, Ulysses Grant, and George B. McClellan.

McClellan supported him to the end, delivering the eulogy at Pickett's funeral in 1875. In the manner of such things, he reached back into history for long-dead heroes to draw comparison with the recently departed. Appropriately, McClellan chose, of all people, Lee's own father as the heroic antecedent for Pickett. Declaimed McClellan, "He will live in history as nearer to Light Horse Harry Lee...than any other of the many heroes produced by Old Virginia."[12] Unwittingly, McClellan had driven to the heart of the problems between Lee and Pickett. It was probably a good thing that neither Lee nor Pickett were around to hear McClellan's words because it is unlikely either would have been flattered by the comparison. Lee might have taken offense at having George Pickett placed in his family tree posthumously.

Pickett might have resented the comparison to a notoriously drunken, dissolute officer whose battlefield reputation was inflated beyond what he deserved. But neither man could have explained why Pickett was really so much like Lighthorse Harry Lee and why that was more of a curse than a blessing in the eyes of Robert E. Lee.

McClellan, who knew Lee and Pickett both quite well, much preferred Pickett, and not just as a boon companion. The two had been in the same class at West Point, and later in Mexico together, which is also where McClellan first made his acquaintance with Lee. He found more to like in Pickett's *bon vivant* nature and cavalier sensibilities than in Lee's Cromwellian austerity—the very same qualities that drove Lee to distraction in his own dealings with Pickett. And after facing Lee in West Virginia in the spring of 1862, McClellan was not overly impressed by Marse Robert's vaunted military prowess either. He wrote to Lincoln that Lee was "too cautious and weak under grave responsibility—personally brave and energetic to a fault, he yet is wanting in moral firmness when pressed by heavy responsibility and is likely to be timid and irresolute in action."[13] McClellan was hardly a shrewd judge of character, as this statement demonstrates, but after facing Lee at Antietam and the Seven Days, and Pickett at Williamsburg and Gaines' Mill, years later he still found it easier to sing Pickett's praises than Lee's. The Pickett he recalled in his eulogy was the popular hero of Pickett's Charge, of San Juan Island and Chapultapec before the Civil War, not the Pickett of Five Forks and Sayler's Creek.

There was more than a little irony to this because Lee had always admired McClellan as a worthy foe. Late in life, when asked who was the greatest of all the Federal commanders he had faced, he answered without hesitation, McClellan. Thus the circle was squared between Lee, McClellan, and Pickett. Since Lee tended to make men like George Pickett and George McClellan uncomfortable, it is no surprise that the two younger men gravitated toward each other and felt similar antipathy toward Lee.[14]

But the crowning irony may have been something that occurred years later. In 1899 a fine oil portrait of George Pickett was presented to the Robert E. Lee Camp of Confederate Veterans by Richard Maury, one of the famous seagoing Maurys whose father had been a classmate of Pickett's at West Point. It was a gift of the George Pickett Confederate Veterans Camp and was accompanied by a stirring presentation speech about the subject's stout-hearted service to the Lost Cause. The portrait was proudly displayed for years in the old veterans' meeting hall, conjuring a relationship which in the popular imagination made them the Charlemagne and Roland of Lost Cause mythology.

A final look at the Lee-Pickett relationship puts to rest one bit of conventional wisdom about Lee and underscores another. It has often been said that Lee followed a *laissez faire* policy toward his officers below corps level. In other words, where a Longstreet or a Jackson or an A.P. Hill were in line for promotion, he was very outspoken about whom he wanted around him, but after choosing his lieutenant generals he relied on his senior officers and the War Department to determine who filled what assignment. This belief is largely a myth. The truth is, Lee took a keen interest in his officers all up and down the chain of command, freely discussing their merits and demerits when called upon to provide his official opinion. The fact that he was so knowledgeable about his officers on all levels is why Jefferson Davis valued his advice so highly when it came to promotions and transfers.[15]

Lee was not averse to reaching down to division or even brigade level to reshuffle his officers corps. Nor did he feel any need to wait for problems to be brought to him; he was proactive in weeding out incompetent officers, even when those officers had powerful friends and personal claims to his affections. Brigadier General Thomas Drayton of South Carolina was a good friend of both Jefferson Davis and Lee. As a brigade commander in D. R. Jones' Division of Longstreet's Corps, however, he was an abject failure who tended to go to pieces under pressure. Lee found him a source of "delay and embarrassment" to the army. On the march his division was disorganized and undisciplined. He failed to display either judgment or leadership at Second Manassas, South Mountain, and Antietam, causing Lee to give up on him completely. Determined to remove Drayton from the army immediately, while admitting that, "He is a gentleman," Lee wrote to the president explaining, "I have endeavored for some time to avoid the necessity of pursuing the course I am now about to take." Lee was able to carefully document each and every one of Drayton's deficiencies, showing a remarkable grasp of detail. The commanding general concluded with, "I am compelled, therefore, to make a change, and wish to do it in the manner least disagreeable to General Drayton, for whom I feel great friendship." Lee's solution was to arrange a thirty days' leave of absence for the hapless brigadier, to give Richmond time to find "some duty...for him in the South or Southwest, which he may be able to perform with advantage to the service." The desired move was made, and after August 1863, Drayton never set foot in Virginia the rest of the war.[16]

The record of the Lee-Pickett relationship, scanty though it may be, shows that Lee took a direct, personal interest in George Pickett, too, starting in the winter of 1863 and continuing right down to the end of the war. After Gettysburg, it is apparent that Lee arranged to have Pickett sent "south" (*cf.* Drayton's case) where he could do little damage but still be of "advantage to the service." The pretext at the time was that Pickett's Division needed to refit and recruit, a realistic explanation except that several other divisions in the army were in equally bad shape, and they continued to serve actively in the field. When Lee dismissed Pickett at the end and sent him home, there was no longer any need to consider his feelings or attempt to find a useful place for him in some other theater. By that time there were no other theaters or alternate service for failed officers.

This brings us to the second point to be learned from a study of this relationship. Unfortunately, Lee's personal relationships with his "lieutenants"—excepting Longstreet and Jackson—as well as his considered opinions of their abilities, are largely uncharted territory for biographers. What thought processes did he go through before promoting or transferring a man? What criteria did he follow in his recommendations? And what did it take to push him to his limits? That he was successful in judging men and getting the most out of them is unquestionable. But Robert E. Lee's brilliant record as a manager of men is usually chalked up more to natural charisma than to a definite philosophy. Even the biographer who literally wrote the book on Lee and his "lieutenants," Douglas Southall Freeman, admitted that this was a side of Lee's character for which there is "little specific information."[17] Yet a careful study of the Pickett-Lee relationship does pull back the curtain just a bit on this aspect of General Lee by showing how he dealt with one particularly troublesome lieutenant. And it opens a new window on George Pickett's record with the Army of Northern Virginia.

Endnotes

Chapter 1:

1. "Immediate family" quoted by Eppa Hunton in "Foreword" of Eppa Hunton, *Autobiography* (Richmond: William Byrd Press, 1933), n. p. For "General Pickett," Hunton, 126.
2. Letter from John S. Mosby to Eppa Hunton, Jr., March 25, 1911. Quoted in Hunton, 127; and in Mosby, "Personal Recollections of General Lee," *Munsey's Magazine*, Vol. 45, No. 1, April, 1911, 69.
3. John B. Jones, *A Rebel War Clerk's Diary at the Confederate States Capital* (Philadelphia: J. B. Lippincott and Co., 1866), Vol. II, 196-97.
4. Helen D. Longstreet, *Lee and Longstreet at High Tide* (Gainesville, GA.: published by author, 1904, reprinted 1988), 54.
5. Glenn Tucker, *Lee and Longstreet at Gettysburg* (Indianapolis, IN: Bobbs-Merrill, 1968), 82.

Chapter 2:

1. Rollin G. Osterweise, quoted in William F. Freehoff, "Southern Sampler" column, *Southern Partisan Magazine*, Vol. XVI, Second Quarter, 1996, 43.
2. The figure 303 comes from *The Register of Graduates and Former Cadets of the United States Military Academy, 1802-1948* (New York: West Point Alumni Foundation, Inc., 1948), 386-87.
3. Quoted in Charles L. Dufour, *The Mexican War: A Compact History, 1846-1848* (New York: Hawthorn Books, 1968), 281.
4. Lee to Annette Carter from Fort Mason, Texas, January 16, 1861, Robert E. Lee Papers, University Library, Washington and Lee University, Lexington, VA.
5. For Pickett, see Mrs. General George E. Pickett, "The Wartime Story of General Pickett," *Cosmopolitan Magazine*, Vol. LVI, No. 1, December, 1913, 38-39. For Lee, see Mosby, "Personal Recollections," 68.
6. R. E. Lee to Mary Lee from Fort Brown, Texas, December 27, 1856, in Lee Family Papers, MSS Collections, Virginia Historical Society, Richmond, VA. Hereafter cited as VAHS.
7. There is a report that Pickett, like Lee, was an early advocate of emancipating and enlisting the slaves in the Confederate army. Lee recommended such a course of action to the Confederate Government in the winter of 1865, while Pickett was said to have favored it as early as 1863. No statement by George or LaSalle

verifies such a claim. See *A Soldier of the Civil War*, by "a member of the Virginia Historical Society" (Cleveland, Ohio: privately printed, 1900), 58.

8. The Confederate Regular Army, established by act of the Confederate Congress on March 6, 1861, and numbering only about 1,750 in its original form, never amounted to a significant force during the war. Pickett was one of the few officers who actually took the oath and was assigned rank in the Regulars. This was partly the result of his unattached status following his late arrival in Richmond. Most fellow officers by the time fighting broke out in April 1861, had already resigned their commissions in the U.S. Army and associated themselves with state forces or volunteer units being raised for service with the Provisional Army of the Confederate States (authorized by the Confederate Congress on February 28, 1861). The Regular Army, C.S.A., was never much more than a concept in the mind of Jefferson Davis. See "Army, Confederate," in Richard N. Current, ed., *Encyclopedia of the Confederacy* (New York: Simon & Schuster, 1993), Vol. 1, 64.
9. For a discussion of icons and "super icons," see Michael T. Marsden, "Iconology of the Western Romance," 284-85; and Gregor Goethels, "Sacred-Secular Icons," 29-30 in *Icons of America*, ed. by Ray Browne and Marshall Fishwick (Bowling Green, OH: Bowling Green State University Popular Press, 1978). See also "Living in the Material World: The Meaning and Power of Popular Icons," in Jack Nachbar and Kevin Lause, eds., *Popular Culture: An Introductory Text* (Bowling Green, OH.: Bowling Green State University Popular Press, 1994), 171-73.
10. G. Moxley Sorrel, *Recollections of a Confederate Staff Officer* (New York: Neale Publishing Co., 1905, reprinted 1978), 54.
11. For Lee, see Charles Bracelen Flood, *Lee: The Last Years* (Boston: Houghton Mifflin Co., 1981), 161. For Pickett, see W. J. Cash, *The Mind of the South* (New York: Alfred A. Knopf, 1965), 121. For "secretive admirer," see *A Soldier of the Civil War*, by "a member of the Virginia Historical Society" 59, 62. For "Bayard of America," see New York *Herald* editorial on the occasion of Lee's death, quoted in Richmond *Daily Whig*, October 15, 1870, n.p. Regarding the Napoleonic connection, an editorialist in the Philadelphia *Press* preferred to see Lee as "rather a Wellington than a Napoleon," unintentionally re-emphasizing the contrast between Lee and Pickett. Quoted in Richmond *Daily Whig*, October 25, 1870, n.p.
12. Lee was never shy about expressing his admiration for officers whom he liked. Indeed, Lee's shrewd appraisal of talent was one of the qualities Jefferson Davis liked most about him. About Henry Heth, Lee wrote the Secretary of War on November 23, 1861, "I would be very glad to have him in any capacity." Lee to Judah P.

Benjamin, November 23, 1861, in U.S. War Department, *The War of the Rebellion: A Compilation of the Official Records of the Union and Confederate Armies* (Washington, DC: U. S. Government Printing Office, 1880-1901), Vol. LIII (Supplement), 191. (hereafter cited as *OR*). Re: A. P. Hill, Lee informed Jefferson Davis in January 1864 that, in effect, he was willing to part with practically any of his senior officers except Hill. James I. Robertson, Jr., General A. P. Hill (New York: Random House, 1987), 247. Re: Lee and Longstreet, see Longstreet, "Lee in Pennsylvania," in A. K. McClure, ed., *The Annals of the War Written by Leading Participants North and South: Originally Published in the Philadelphia Weekly Times* (Philadelphia: Times Publishing Co., 1879, reprinted, 1988), 433 (hereafter cited as *Annals of the War*).

13. The almost mythic bond between Jackson and Lee was captured on canvas by St. Louis artist Everett B. D. Julio in his popular 1869 painting, *The Last Meeting of Lee and Jackson*, purporting to show the final war council between the two commanders just before their moment of greatest triumph. For a deeper discussion of the relationship of Jackson and Lee, see Joseph T. Glatthaar, *Partners in Command* (New York: The Free Press, 1994), 28 ff. For the same on Davis and Lee, see Steven E. Woodworth, *Davis & Lee at War* (Lawrence, KS: University Press of Kansas, 1995).
14. Dixon Wector, *The Hero in America: A Chronicle of Hero Worship* (New York: Charles Scribner's Sons, 1941), 301.

Chapter 3:

1. Douglas Southall Freeman, *Lee's Lieutenants: A Study in Command* (New York: Charles Scribner's Sons, 1942, 1944), Vol. II, 665.
2. Quoting Alexander Cheves Haskell, unpublished manuscript, Southern Historical Collection, Wilson Library, University of North Carolina at Chapel Hill. (Cited in Everand H. Smith, ed., "As They Saw General Lee," *Civil War Times Illustrated*, October, 1986), 22.
3. Hunton, 113. Porter Alexander, *Military Memoirs of a Confederate: A Critical Narrative* (New York: Charles Scribner's Sons, 1907, reprinted, 1962), 503. Charles Marshall, *An Aide-de-Camp of Lee*, ed. by Sir Frederick Maurice (Boston: Little, Brown, and Company, 1927), xxv-xxvi (Introduction). For testimony to Lee's sour disposition late in the war, see, Emory Thomas, *Robert E. Lee, A Biography* (New York: W. W. Norton & Co., 1995), 350-52.
4. These are the qualities that Lee saw in Stonewall Jackson and A. P. Hill in particular that he valued so highly. See *OR*, Vol. XIX, Pt. 2, 643. (See also Freeman, *Lee's Lieutenants*, 247.)
5. Mary D. and William S. McFeely, *Ulysses S. Grant, Memoirs and Selected Letters* (New York: The Library of America, reprint, 1990), 598.
6. Sorrel, 54.

7. Walter Taylor, *General Lee, His Campaigns in Virginia, 1861-65 With Personal Reminiscences* (Norfolk, VA.: Nusbaum, 1906, reprint, 1975), 157.
8. The first followed the Seven Days battles, when Lee first made the army his own. Lee carried out a "quiet revolution" in the army's command structure with supreme tact and "manifest regard for merit," creating in the process the basic corps organization. Under Longstreet and Jackson now were six divisional commanders. See Freeman, *Lee's Lieutenants*, Vol. II, 670-74.
9. See Marcus J. Wright, compiler, *General Officers of the Confederate Army, Officers of the Executive Departments of the Confederate States, Members of the Confederate Congress by States* (New York: Neale Publishing Co., 1911, reprint, 1983), 14-15; and Freeman, *Lee's Lieutenants*, Vol. II, 247-48.
10. *Ibid.*, 264.
11. *OR,* Vol. XIX, Pt. 2, 681-82, 683.
12. Freeman, *Lee's Lieutenants*, Vol. II, 266. (Footnote no. 71).
13. *OR,* Vol. XIX, Pt. 2, 698.
14. For evaluations of Ewell and Hill, see Donald C. Pfanz, "Richard Stoddert Ewell," in *The Confederate General* (Harrisburg, PA: National Historical Society, 1991), Vol. 2, 111-12; and James I. Robertson, "Ambrose Powell Hill," Ibid., Vol. 3, 96-98. For Lee quote, see R. E. Lee to Jefferson Davis, May 20, 1863, *OR,* Vol. XXV, Pt. 2, 810.
15. *OR,* Vol. XXV, Pt. 2, 811. For the case for and against Harvey Hill and Lafayette McLaws, see Freeman, *Lee's Lieutenants*, Vol. II, 694-95.
16. For Theophilus Holmes' less-than-ringing endorsement at the time Pickett was promoted to brigadier, see George E. Pickett to Samuel Cooper, December 28, 1861, *OR,* Vol. LI, Pt. 2, 428. Nor is there any mention in the *OR* of Joe Johnston ever recommending Pickett for promotion during the brief time Pickett fought under his command in the spring of 1862. When Beauregard as department commander arrived at Petersburg on May 10, 1864, to oppose Ben Butler's landing at Bermuda Hundred, one of his first actions was to replace Pickett, currently commanding at Petersburg, with Major General W. H. C. Whiting.
17. Robert E. Lee to James Longstreet, January 19, 1863, in Robert E. Lee Headquarters Papers, MSS Collections, VAHS, Richmond.
18. Col. Stuart to wife in William A. Young, Jr., and Patricia C. Young, *56th Virginia Infantry* (Lynchburg, VA: H. E. Howard, 1990), 74.
19. R. E. Lee to James Longstreet, March 30, 1863, in *OR,* Vol. XVIII, 906-07. For Lee's unconcern about any threat posed by the Federal presence on the coast below Richmond, see Lee to the Secretary of War, January 5, 1863, in *OR,* Vol. XVIII, 819-20.

20. For Hill to North Carolina, see R. E. Lee to the Secretary of War, January 5, 1863, in *O.R.* Vol. XVIII, 819-20. For Pickett's transfer, see Lee to James A. Seddon, February 14, 1863, and Seddon to Lee, February 15, 1863, in *Ibid.*, 876-78. See also Lee to Gustavus Smith, January 4, 1863; Lee to Seddon, January 5, 1863; and Lee to Jefferson Davis, January 6, 1863, in Dowdey and Manarin, *Wartime Papers of Robert E. Lee*, 383, 385-88. For Lee's criticism of Pickett and his division, see R. E. Lee to James Longstreet, January 19, 1863, Robert E. Lee Papers, MSS Collections, VAHS, Richmond. For a good summary of Lee's thinking in this situation, see Woodworth, 215.
21. R. E. Lee to James Longstreet, February 18, 1863, in *OR,* Vol. XXV, Pt. 2, 632.
22. Samuel Cooper, Adj. and Inspector General, to George E. Pickett, February 18, 1863, *OR,* Vol. XVIII, 884.
23. Walter Harrison, *Pickett's Men*, 73.
24. R. E. Lee to James A. Seddon, February 16, 1863, *OR,* Vol. XVIII, 880; Samuel Cooper, Adj. and Inspector Gen., to George E. Pickett, February 18, 1863, *ibid.*, 884; and John Withers, Assistant Adjutant-General, to G. E. Pickett, Special Orders No. 44, February 21, 1863, *ibid.*, 889.
25. Lesley Jill Gordon, "Before the Storm: The Early Life of George E. Pickett," Honors Thesis submitted for B.A. in History, College of William and Mary (Williamsburg, VA), 1987, 94-95.
26. R. E. Lee to James A. Seddon, February 14, 1863, *OR,* Vol. XVIII, 876-77. For Lee's strategic thinking, see Woodworth, 217 ff.
27. R. E. Lee to James A. Seddon, Secretary of War, February 14, 1863, in *OR,* Vol. XXV, Pt. 2, 623. The same point is made by Maj. General Samuel G. French, who was commanding the Dept. of Southern Virginia at the time. See *Two Wars: An Autobiography of General Samuel G. French* (Nashville, TN: Confederate Veteran, 1901), 176.
28. Sorrel, 155-56.
29. See James A. Seddon to Robert E. Lee, April 6, 1863, *OR,* Vol. XXV, Pt. 2, 708-09; also Lee to Samuel Cooper, April 16, 1863 in Clifford Dowdey and Louis H. Manarin, eds., *The Wartime Papers of R. E. Lee* (New York: Bramhall, 1961), 434.
30. Special Orders, May 4, 1863, *OR,* Vol. XVIII, 1045.
31. Jones, Diary, Vol. I, 325.
32. On May 16, Lee informed Longstreet from Richmond that Pickett had passed through the capital that morning on the way up to Hanover Junction, in accordance with orders issued by the Secretary of War. *OR,* Vol. XXV, Pt. 2, 802 (Special Orders No. 116); and "Lee's Telegraph Book," in Lee's Headquarters Papers, MSS Collections, VAHS, Richmond.

33. See Pickett to Major General Arnold Elzey, June 2, 1863, *OR,* Vol. XVIII, 1090-91.
34. Sorrel, 156.
35. All direct quotations above are from Pickett to Elzey, June 2, 1863, *OR,* Vol. XVIII, 1090-91.
36. *Ibid.*
37. *Ibid.*
38. R. E. Lee to George E. Pickett, June 3, 1863, in *OR,* Vol. XXV, Pt. 2, 852-53.
39. *Ibid.*
40. Lee to A. P. Hill, June 8, 1863, *OR,* Vol. XXVII, Pt. 3, 869.
41. J. J. Pettigrew to Arnold Elzey, June 6, 1863, *OR,* Vol. XXV, Pt. 2, 862.
42. R. E. Lee to "Mr. President," in *OR,* Vol. XXVII, Pt. 2, 293; and Lee to Davis (telegram), in Douglas S. Freeman, and Grady McWhiney, eds., *Lee's Dispatches: Unpublished Letters of General Robert E. Lee, C. S. A., to Jefferson Davis, 1862-1865* (New York: G. P. Putnam's Sons, 1957, rev. ed.), 101-2. See also George E. Pickett to Brig. Gen. R. H. Chilton, June 21, 1863, in *OR,* Vol. XXVII, Pt. 3, 910.

Chapter 4:

1. Strictly speaking, Pickett's Division, even reduced by two brigades, was not the weakest, i.e., smallest, in the army. Jubal Early's Division, at 5460 was smaller than Pickett's at 5473, albeit by an insignificant number. John W. Busey and David G. Martin, *Regimental Strengths and Losses at Gettysburg* (Hightstown, New Jersey: Longstreet House, 1994), 283, 286. For Pickett's complaint to headquarters, see Pickett to R. H. Chilton (Adjt. and Insp. Gen., Army of Northern Virginia), June 21, 1863, in *OR,* Vol. XXVII, Pt. 3, 910.
2. Taylor to Pickett, June 29, 1863, *OR,* Vol. XXVII, 944-45.
3. R. E. Lee to General Samuel Cooper, June 23, 1863, in *OR,* Vol. XXVII, Pt. 2, 925-26. For Davis' response explaining why the brigades were being held back, see Davis to Lee, June 28, 1863, in *OR,* Vol. XXVII, Pt. 1, 76-77.
4. George Pickett to LaSalle, June 24, 1863, in *George E. Pickett, The Heart of a Soldier: As Revealed in the Intimate Letters of General George E. Pickett, C.S.A.*, ed. by LaSalle Pickett (New York: Seth Moyle, Inc., 1913), 81.
5. Kathleen Georg and John W. Busey, *Nothing But Glory: Pickett's Division at Gettysburg* (Hightstown, New Jersey: Longstreet House, 1987), 5.
6. General Order No. 72, June 21, 1863, *OR,* Vol. XXVII, Pt. 3, 912-13. (These orders were received by most of the troops three days later.)

7. During the Antietam Campaign the previous year, Lee had ordered a soldier in the Second Corps shot for violating his strict anti-looting rules, so no one doubted that Lee meant business this time. See H. David Williams, "The Glory of War," *Civil War Magazine*, Vol. IX, June, 1987, 18. Colonel Robert M. Powell of the 5th Texas Infantry is quoted in Gregory A. Coco, *Recollections of a Texas Colonel at Gettysburg* (Gettysburg: Thomas Publications, 1990), 9.
8. Garnett to Mrs. Dandridge, June 25, 1863, cited in Georg and Busey, 7-8; "We are not obliged. . ." from Captain H. T. Owen, "Stories of Pickett's Men," Gettysburg Newspaper Cuttings Book No. 6, 28, Gettysburg National Military Park Library.
9. Francis W. Dawson, *Reminiscences of Confederate Service, 1861-1865*, edited by Bell I. Wiley (Baton Rouge: Louisiana State University Press, 1980 reprint of 1882 edition), 91. For testimony to Lee's sense of humor, see Taylor, *General Lee*, 157. For stepping aside to let Hill's brigades pass, see Georg and Busey, 5-6.
10. Douglas Southall Freeman, *R. E. Lee: A Biography* (New York: Charles Scribner's Sons, 1935), Vol. I, 414-15.
11. James Longstreet, "Lee in Pennsylvania," *The Annals of the War*, 419.
12. The linking of Pickett's fate with John Imboden's seems more than mere coincidence. Both sorely disappointed Lee on the Gettysburg campaign. Like Pickett, Imboden was assigned to bring up the rear on the advance into Pennsylvania, and on the retreat after Gettysburg, Imboden was assigned to escort the wagons and ambulances in conjunction with Pickett who was guarding the masses of Federal prisoners captured in the battle. Earlier in the campaign Imboden had attracted Lee's displeasure by taking his brigade off on an unauthorized rest at Hancock, Maryland, without informing the commanding general. In the fall of 1864 Imboden was relieved of command following his questionable actions during Early's Valley Campaign. The rumored reason was "inefficiency." See Freeman, *Lee's Lieutenants*, Vol. 3, 568, 575. "Picking cherries" comes from the diary of Sergeant Levin C. Gayle, June 27, 1863 (typescript), vertical files in Gettysburg National Military Park Library.
13. One has only to cite the example of Longstreet's "secret" march along Herr Ridge on the second day at Gettysburg. He ordered Hood's and McLaws' Divisions to march to the right flank of the Confederate lines preparatory to launching an attack on the Peach Orchard. When the troops were forced to countermarch in order to avoid detection by Yankee observers on Little Round Top, McLaws insisted on keeping the "point of honor" at the head of the column despite throwing the entire movement into disarray and delaying the attack for hours. For a fuller discussion of Longstreet's march

and countermarch on July 2, see Edwin B. Coddington, *The Gettysburg Campaign: A Study in Command* (Dayton, Ohio: Morningside Bookshop, 1983), 377-80.

14. For "Tell General Pickett," see Harrison, 88. For discussion of Pickett's tardy arrival on the field, see Jeffrey D. Wert, *General James Longstreet* (New York: Simon & Schuster, 1993), 282.
15. Harrison, 91-92.
16. Longstreet, "Lee in Pennsylvania," *The Annals of the War*, 429.
17. *Ibid.*, 429.
18. Captain James R. Hutter, 11th Virginia Infantry Regiment, to John W. Daniel, n.d., John W. Daniel Papers, Box 23, Special Collections, Alderman Library, University of Virginia, Charlottesville, VA.
19. Diary of Sgt. Levin C. Gayle, Vertical Files, Gettysburg National Military Park Library, Gettysburg, PA. W. W. Wood, "Pickett's Charge at Gettysburg," Philadelphia *Times*, August 11, 1877, n.p.
20. Sorrel, 54.
21. James H. Walker, "A Survivor of Pickett's Division," in *Gettysburg*, Booklet No. 282 (Suffolk, VA.: Robert Hardy Publications, privately printed, n.d.), 11.
22. See Lee's Report, *OR,* Vol. XXVII, Pt. 2, 320.
23. The first-hand observations of General Lee on July 3 come from five different witnesses: Prussian Captain Justus Scheibert and Colonel R. Lindsay Walker of the Confederate artillery, in Jubal Early, J. William Jones, et al, eds., *Southern Historical Society Papers* (Richmond: Southern Historical Society), Vol. V (Jan.-Dec., 1880), 92 and 181. Hereafter cited as *SHSP*; Longstreet, "Lee in Pennsylvania," *The Annals of the War*, 433; General John Bell Hood, *Advance and Retreat: Personal Experiences in the United States and Confederate States Armies* (New Orleans: Hood Orphan Memorial Fund, 1880, reprint 1959), 57; and Captain of Engineers W. W. Blackford, *War Years with Jeb Stuart* (New York: Charles Scribner's Sons, 1945), 230. For "General Lee's Face," see John Dooley, *John Dooley, Confederate Soldier. His War Journal*, ed. by Joseph T. Durkin (New York: Georgetown University Press, 1945), 101.
24. Rumors of a broad attack along the entire front were widespread in the army on the morning of July 3. George Pickett heard it from Porter Alexander, who as designated commander of the artillery bombardment, would certainly be expected to be privy to the master plan. See Alexander, *Military Memoirs of a Confederate*, 422; also George Pickett to LaSalle, July [?], 1863, in *George Pickett, Soldier of the South: General Pickett's War Letters to His Wife*, Arthur Crew Inman, ed. (Boston: Houghton Mifflin Company, 1928), 69.
25. The picture of Pickett's mood swing comes from his letter of July 3 to LaSalle Corbell—entrusted to Longstreet just before the Charge—in Pickett, *The Heart of a Soldier*, 96. Although the ve-

racity of this collection of letters has been called into question on numerous points by myself and others, there is no reason to suspect that this particular portion of the famous "Farewell Letter" was fabricated or doctored by a later editor. This segment at least has verisimilitude.

26. According to Major James E. Dearing, Pickett's chief of artillery. Cited in Earl Schenck Miers and Richard Brown, eds., *Gettysburg* (New Brunswick, New Jersey: Rutgers University Press, 1948), 230.
27. For "shot down" and other criticism of Lee, see Private William A. Fletcher, Company F, 5th Texas Infantry (Hood's Division), in *Fletcher, Rebel Private: Front and Rear; Memoirs of a Confederate Soldier* (New York: Dutton Books, 1995 reprint of 1908 edition), 84.
28. Comte de Paris, *The Battle of Gettysburg: From the History of the Civil War in America* (Philadelphia: Porter & Coates, 1886, reprinted 1987), 218.
29. In Pickett's Division, six colonels of regiments were killed outright on the field—Hodges, Edmonds, Magruder, Williams, Patton, and Allen. Two more colonels were mortally wounded—Owens and Stuart. Three lieutenant colonels were killed—Calcott, Wade, and Ellis. Five colonels were wounded—Hunton, Terry, Garnett, Mayo, and Aylett—and four lieutenant colonels commanding regiments were also wounded—Carrington, Otey, Richardson, and Martin. Of the whole compliment of field officers in fifteen regiments only one, Lieutenant Col. Joseph C. Cabell, escaped unhurt. These casualties were on top of the three brigadiers—Kemper, Garnett, and Armistead—who were killed or, in Kemper's case, severely wounded.
30. Historian Monroe F. Cockrell says, "That Pickett did not "go through" seems to have been well known to many officers in both armies who were present at the battle." Cockrell, "Where Was Pickett at Gettysburg?", typescript (1949) in Alderman Library, University of Virginia at Charlottesville, 13. See also Judge John Purifoy of Alabama, quoted in Walter Geer, *Campaigns of the Civil War* (New York: Brenatno's, 1926), who says, "No one saw Pickett lead this charge, and no one ever saw anybody who did."
31. The first episode occurred at the Battle of the Wilderness, when Lee determined to lead the Texas Brigade into action. It was subsequently described in their memoirs by Porter Alexander and Charles Venable, both of whom were present that day. The Spotsylvania episode less than a week later is likewise described by John B. Gordon and A. L. Long in their memoirs, although Long says it occurred twice (May 10 and 11), thus giving the possibility of not two but three separate episodes of "Lee to the rear!" Porter Alexander, *Fighting for the Confederacy*, ed. by Gary Gallagher (Chapel Hill: University of North Carolina Press, 1989), 358.

Charles Venable, "General Lee in the Wilderness Campaign," in *B & L*, Robert U. Johnson and Clarence C. Buell, eds. (New York: Century Co., 1887-88, reprinted 1956), Vol. IV, 241. Hereafter cited as *B & L*. John B. Gordon, *Reminiscences of the Civil War* (New York: Charles Scribner's Sons, 1904), 278-79. A. L. Long, *Memoirs of Robert E. Lee: His Military and Personal History* (Secaucus, New Jersey, 1983 reprint of 1886 edition), 341. For Jefferson Davis and Lee, see Davis, "Jefferson Davis Remembers Robert E. Lee," *North American Review*, Vol. CL (1890), 55.

32. Long, *Memoirs*, 341.
33. Dawson, *Reminiscences of Confederate Service*, 96-97.
34. William T. Poague, *Gunner with Stonewall*, ed. by Monroe F. Cockrell (Jackson, TN: McCowat-Mercer Press, 1957), 253-54.
35. Two slightly different versions of this famous encounter have come down to us, the first by Pickett's staff officer, Robert A. Bright, and the second by Corporal Charles T. Loehr of the First Virginia Infantry. Loehr's account does not include the bitter exchange between Lee and Pickett, but does better describing the little personal things each man did in that dramatic moment when they came face to face, such as crying and shaking hands. See Robert A. Bright, "Pickett's Charge: The Story of It as Told by a Member of His Staff," *SHSP*, Vol. XXI (Jan.-Dec., 1903), 228; and Loehr, "The 'Old First' Virginia at Gettysburg," *SHSP*, Vol. XXXII (Jan./Dec.,1904), 37. There is another famous example of the "Lee handshake," involving James Longstreet, just after the Battle of Sharpsburg/Antietam. See Freeman, *R. E. Lee*, Vol. II, 403.
36. Anonymous quotation in James V. Murfin, *The Gleam of Bayonets* (Cranbury, New Jersey: Thomas Yoseloff, 1965), 291. The story is attributed elsewhere to General Stephen D. Lee. See Jerry W. Holsworth, "Uncommon Valor: Hood's Texas Brigade in the Maryland Campaign," *Blue & Gray Magazine*, Vol. XIII, No. 6, August, 1996, 54-55.
37. Loehr, "The 'Old First' Virginia at Gettysburg," 37, explicated in Georg and Busey, 185-86.
38. Sorrel, 173. Arthur J. L. Fremantle, *Three Months in the Southern States: April-June, 1863* (Edinburgh, Scotland: W. Blackwood and Sons, 1991 reprint of 1863 edition), 268-69.

Chapter 5:

1. General Orders No. 74, Headquarters, Army of Northern Virginia, July 4, 1863, in *OR*, Vol. XXVII, Pt. 2, 311.
2. *Ibid.*
3. Pickett told LaSalle from Williamsport that "more than a fourth of my division have been placed hors de combat." George Pickett to

LaSalle Corbell, July 8, 1863, in *Soldier of the South*, 66. As a matter of fact, Pickett's division had lost 2,904 men in the Charge, or about 53.1% of its strength. By contrast, Heth's and Rodes' Divisions lost more men at Gettysburg (3,358 and 3,116 respectively), but a lower percentage of their total strength (45.0% and 39.0% respectively. Figures come from *The Civil War Book of Lists* (Conshohocken, PA: Combined Books, 1993), 70-71. See also the Army of Northern Virginia's "Monthly Return for July," which shows Pickett's effective total present at the end of the month as 3,316. *OR,* Vol. XXVII, Pt. 2, 292.

4. George Pickett to LaSalle Corbell, July 6, 1863, *Soldier of the South*, 64-65, 75.
5. See R. E. Lee to Maj. Gen. George E. Pickett, July 8, 1863 (in response to letter of July 7th), *OR,* Vol. XXVII, Pt. 3, 983.
6. R. E. Lee to Major General George E. Pickett, July 9, 1863, *OR,* Vol. XXVII, Pt. 3, 987. George Pickett to LaSalle Corbell, July 12, 1863, *Soldier of the South*, 75.
7. Lee reassigned Iverson's Brigade to Dodson Ramseur's command by Sp. Orders No. 173 (July 10) and relieved him of command by Sp. Orders No. 175 (July 16), the latter action being subsequently rescinded by Jefferson Davis. See *OR,* Vol. XXVII, Pt. 3, 993 and 1016.
8. George Pickett to LaSalle Corbell, July [?], 1863, in *Soldier of the South* 69-71.
9. Freeman, *R. E. Lee*, Vol. III, 331.
10. R. E. Lee to George E. Pickett, July 9, 1863, in *OR,* Vol. XXVII, Pt. 3, 986-87.
11. ”Unfortunate” quoted by Justus Scheibert, *Seven Months in the Rebel States During the North American War, 1863*, (Tuscaloosa: University of Alabama Press, 1958 reprint of 1875 edition), 208. "Invincible" quoted in Paddy Griffith, *Battle Tactics of the Civil War* (New Haven: Yale University Press, 1989), 142-43.
12. *OR,* Vol. XXVII, Pt. 3, 986.
13. August 10, 1863, in Freeman and McWhiney,119-20.
14. George Pickett to "Sallie" Corbell, July 23, 1863, in Pickett, *Soldier of the South*, 78.
15. James Longstreet, "Lee's Right Wing at Gettysburg," *B & L*, Vol. III, 349.
16. Walter Taylor, *Four Years with General Lee* (New York: D. Appleton and Co., 1877, reprint,1962), 77.
17. For "casualties," see R. E. Lee to George Pickett in *OR,* Vol. XXVII, Pt. 3, 1075. For "Lee's wishes," see Pickett, *The Heart of a Soldier*, 213 ("Editorial Note").
18. Pickett's final report of his operations is contained in Harrison, 149-50.

19. Both quotes are from Walter Taylor, not George Pickett, but they contain sentiments that Pickett expressed in his letters, either explicitly or implicitly, on other occasions. See Walter Taylor, *Lee's Adjutant: The Wartime Letters of Colonel Walter Herron Taylor, 1862-1865*, ed. by R. Lockwood Tower with John S. Belmont (Columbia: University of South Carolina Press, 1995), 68, 182.
20. Wilcox's original after-action report, dated July 17, 1863, from Bunker Hill, VA. is in the *OR,* Vol. XXVII, Pt. 2, 617-21. For "uncensored" version, dated simply "July/63," see R. E. Lee, Headquarters Papers, VAHS, Richmond. That report is reproduced in Freeman, *R. E. Lee*, Vol. III, 554-56.
21. Marshall, 180.
22. R. E. Lee to General Samuel Cooper, July 31, 1863, in *OR,* Vol. XXVII, Pt. 2, 305-11; and Lee to Cooper, January [?], 1864, *ibid.*, 313-25.
23. R. E. Lee to Jefferson Davis, August 8, 1863, Dowdey and Manarin, 589-90; and Davis to Lee in *OR,* Vol. XXIX, Pt. 2, 640.
24. Brown, "Lee at Gettysburg: The Man, the Myth, the Recriminations," 50.
25. Lee to Cooper, July 31, 1863, 320; and James Longstreet, *From Manassas to Appomattox: Memoirs of the Civil War in America* (Philadelphia: J. B. Lippincott Co., 1896, reprinted with editing by James I. Robertson by Indiana University Press, 1960), 388.
26. See in particular, Robert A. Bright, "Pickett's Charge: The Story of It as Told by a Member of His Staff," in Richmond *Times-Dispatch*, February 7, 1904, Sec. 3, p. 2; and Thomas R. Friend, "Pickett's Position: Where the General Was During the Battle of Gettysburg," Letter to the Editor, Richmond *Times-Dispatch*, November 24, 1903, Sec. 3, p. 4.

Chapter 6:

1. "Misconduct" was Brigadier General Dodson Ramseur's choice of words. For that and "went to pieces," see Coddington, 289-90, 696 (fnt. 19). For Iverson's after-action report and Lee's official actions, see *OR,* Vol. XXVII, Pt. 2, 578-81; and *OR,* Vol. XXVII, Pt. 3, 993, 1016. See also Daniel Bauer, "'The Most Conspicuous Failure': The Slaughter of the North Carolina Brigade on Gettysburg's First Day," *Civil War Magazine*, Vol. XVII (1989), 14; and Lawrence L. Hewitt, "Alfred Iverson, Jr." entry in *The Confederate General*, ed. by William C. Davis (Harrisburg, PA: National Historical Society, 1991), Vol. 3, 142-43.
2. Freeman and McWhiney, xxiii (Introduction).
3. For "capable officers," see R. E. Lee to "Mr. President," January 27, 1864, in *OR,* Vol. XXXIII, 1124-25. At the time Longstreet was wounded, Pickett was the second ranking major general in the First

Corps behind Richard H. Anderson, whose promotion dated from July 14, 1862, three months before Pickett's. For an account of how the decision was made, see Sorrel, 248.

4. Sorrel, 248.
5. See R. E. Lee to Maj. Gen. George E. Pickett, January 20, 1864, in *OR,* Vol. XXXIII, 1102-3. "New Berne" was the preferred mid-19th century spelling of the town's name, so that is the spelling that is used in the present work.
6. John G. Barrett, *The Civil War in North Carolina* (Chapel Hill: University of North Carolina Press, 1963), 203.
7. Lee to Pickett, January 20, 1864, in *OR,* Vol. XXXIII, 1102-3.
8. Sorrel, 54-55.
9. For Pickett's after-action report and cover letter to Lee, see G. E. Pickett to General R. E. Lee, February 15, 1864, in *OR,* Vol. XXXIII, 92-94. This report, without the cover letter, is also found in "Operations against Newbern in 1864, Report of General Pickett, February 15, 1864," in *SHSP*, Vol. IX (1881), 1-4.
10. For the correspondence between Hoke and Lee, and Lee and Pickett, see R. F. Hoke to Major Walter Taylor, February 8, 1864, in *OR,* Vol. XXXIII, 95-97; and R. E. Lee to Major General George E. Pickett, February 18, 1864, *ibid.*, 1186-87. For court of inquiry, see Freeman and McWhiney, 136-37 (Fnt. 2); also, Robert G. H. Kean, *Inside the Confederate Government: The Diary of Robert Garlick Hill Kean*, ed. by Edward Younger (New York: Oxford University Press, 1957), 151. For Lee's note to Hoke, see Barrett, *The Civil War in North Carolina*, 207.
11. R. E. Lee to General G. E. Pickett, April 11, 1864, in *OR,* Vol. XXXIII, 1273-74.
12. Kean, *Inside the Confederate Government*, 445.
13. R. Lockwood Tower, ed., *Lee's Adjutant: The Wartime Letters of Colonel Walter Herron Taylor, 1862-1865* (Columbia, South Carolina: University of South Carolina Press, 1995), 21.
14. Fayetteville [Tennessee] *Observer*, May 24, 1863, 3. Quoted in *Robert G. Hartje, Van Dorn: The Life and Times of a Confederate General* (Nashville, TN.: Vanderbilt University Press, 1967, 318.
15. LaSalle Pickett, *Pickett and His Men*, 322.
16. John B. Jones, *A Rebel War Clerk's Diary*, ed. by Howard Swiggett (New York: Old Hickory Bookshop, 1935), Vol. II, 165-66.
17. Lee to R. H. Anderson, *OR,* Vol. LI, Pt. 2, 1019. Original in E. P. Alexander Papers, File 19, June, 13-30, 1864, MSS. Dept., Southern Historical Collection, Wilson Library, University of North Carolina at Chapel Hill. See also "Address by Richard L. Maury to Lee Camp, C.V.," June 9, 1899, in Special Collections, William R. Perkins Library, Duke University, Durham, NC; and in Harrison, 130-31.

18. George E. Pickett to Robert E. Lee, May 21, 1864, in James William Eldridge Collection, Box 46, MSS Dept., Huntington Library, San Marino, CA.
19. George Pickett to "Sallie" Pickett, July 17, 1864, in Arthur Crew Inman Papers, Box II, File 40, John Marshall Library, Brown University, Providence, Rhode Island. Unlike most other Pickett letters where LaSalle's heavy editorial hand is suspected, this letter in its original, hand-written form is not a typescript. "Never seek" from Thomas, 18.
20. G. E. Pickett to Col. G. M. Sorrel, May 28, 1864, *OR,* Vol. XXXVI, Pt. 3, 843-44.
21. Robert E. Lee to Lieutenant General James Longstreet, January 19, 1865, Fairfax Papers, MSS Collections, VAHS, Richmond.
22. Jones, condensed, edited, and annotated by Earl Schenck Miers (New York: Sagamore Press, Inc., 1958), 454 (referred to hereafter as *War Clerk's Diary*, Miers, ed.).
23. Dispatch No. 211 from Lee's Headquarters, August 13, 1864, in Freeman and McWhiney, 369.
24. John Reagan quoted in Mark E. Neely, Jr. and Harold Holzer, "The Miserable First Ladies," *Civil War Magazine*, Vol. XXI, 13. All other quotes in paragraph from Jones, 454.
25. Jones, 454.
26. Charles Pickett to Richard L. Maury ("My Dear Dick"), March 5, 1894, in Richard L. Maury Papers, Duke University.
27. The "mobile reserve" explanation was preferred by Douglas S. Freeman, while admitting that the arrangement was "somewhat mystifying." See Freeman, *Lee's Lieutenants*, Vol. III, 627. Likewise, Lee biographer Clifford Dowdey also saw Pickett's Division in the role of a "fire brigade" during the Petersburg siege. Clifford Dowdey, *Lee's Last Campaign* (Boston: Little Brown & Co., 1960), 336.

Chapter 7:

1. After further reflection, Grant decided he was ready to "end the matter," and instructed Sheridan to "push around the enemy if you can and get on his right rear." *OR,* Vol. XLVI, Pt. 3, 266. See also Philip H. Sheridan, *Personal Memoirs of P. H. Sheridan* (New York: D. Appleton and Co., 1888), Vol. 2, 139-40.
2. McFeely, 697-98.
3. Although conventional wisdom, based on LaSalle Pickett's reminiscences, ascribes Lee's "Hold at all hazards" directive to special orders issued on March 31, no copy of such orders has been found. It is more logical to believe that Lee used this council of March 30 to impart that particular message to Pickett, although perhaps not in those exact words. If the special orders in question were indeed issued on March 31, they probably only reconfirmed the previous

message. See note #128. An account of the March 30th war-council-in-the-rain is provided by Thomas Conolly. One of the last foreigners to enter the Confederacy, Conolly was a British M. P. who slipped through the blockade in February, 1865 to offer his services to the beleaguered nation, and stayed until the end. See Thomas Conolly, *An Irishman in Dixie: Thomas Conolly's Diary of the Fall of the Confederacy*, ed. by Nelson D. Lankford (Columbia: University of South Carolina Press, 1988), 74-76.

4. Horace Porter, "Five Forks and the Pursuit of Lee," *B & L*, Vol. 4, 711.
5. The original copy of these orders no longer exists. However, they are cited by LaSalle Pickett in *Pickett and His Men*, 386, and endorsed by Freeman in *Lee's Lieutenants*, Vol. III, 661.
6. During this same period, Grant was likewise in the dark about Sheridan's whereabouts, but as the commanding general informed his headquarters on April 2, "I have not yet heard from Sheridan, but I have an abiding faith that he is in the right place and at the right time." Lee had no such "abiding faith" in his own subordinate. See U. S. Grant to Col. T. S. Bowers in *OR,* Vol. XLVI, Pt. 3, 449. (Bowers was Assistant Adjutant General at City Point, Virginia.)
7. Harrison cites as evidence the full text of Pickett's final report to Lee, which was based solely on Pickett's recollections at the end of the war, without any corresponding documentation in the Official Records. Harrison accepted Pickett's version unquestioningly, as do most modern scholars, albeit not without reservations. See Harrison, 145; see also Lee's summation of Pickett's report in "Lee to Breckenridge," *OR,* Vol. XLVI, Pt. 1, 1263-64; and discussion of same in Freeman, *Lee's Lieutenants*, Vol. III, 662.
8. Sheridan, *Memoirs*, Vol. 2, 161.
9. Lee to Breckenridge, April 1, 1865, in Dowdey and Manarin, 923.
10. Lee to Breckenridge, April 2, 1865, *ibid.*, 924-25.
11. Otto Eisenschiml and E. B. Long, *As Luck Would Have It; Chance and Coincidence in the Civil War* (Indianapolis: Bobbs-Merrill, 1948), 256.
12. Lee to Davis, August 13, 1864, in Freeman and McWhiney, 369.
13. General Warren was summarily relieved of command by Philip Sheridan after the Battle of Five Forks, ostensibly for dilatoriness and failure to obey orders during the April 1 attack on Pickett's lines. Thus, Five Forks led directly to the ruining of two prominent military careers among general officers. For details of Warren's dismissal, see Emerson Gifford Taylor, *Gouverneur Kemble Warren: Life and Letters of an American Soldier* (Gaithersburg, MD: Ron Van Sickle Military Books, 1988 reprint of 1932 edition), 207-48.

14. Tom Rosser, Philadelphia *Weekly Times*, April 5, 1885, n.p. Davis, "Jefferson Davis Remembers Robert E. Lee," *North American Review*, Vol. CL, 1890, 63.
15. Randolph H. McKim, The Soul of Lee (New York: Longmans, Green and Co., 1918), 125.
16. McKim, 101; Tom Rosser, letter to Philadelphia *Weekly Times*, April 5, 1885, n.p.
17. Dowdey and Manarin, 923.
18. Otto Eisenschiml and E. B. Long, *As Luck Would Have It* (New York: Bobbs-Merrill Company, 1948), 250.
19. Hunton, 122.
20. Henry A. Wise, "The Career of Wise's Brigade," *SHSP*, Vol. XXV, 17-18. Also cited in Burke Davis, *To Appomattox: Nine April Days, 1865* (Washington, DC: Eastern Acorn Press, 1981), 41; and Richard Wayne Lykes, *The Campaign for Petersburg* (Washington, DC: National Park Service, n.d.), 66.
21. Wise, Vol. XXV, 19. Freeman says this scene was witnessed by his father and others, citing it in both *R. E. Lee*, Vol. IV, 96f, and *Lee's Lieutenants*, Vol. III, 714f. Both Freeman and descendants of the Wise family believed that General Wise's remark was aimed specifically at Bushrod Johnson who was in the vicinity at the time. Whomever it was aimed at directly, it certainly applied to George Pickett, and Henry Wise was no Pickett admirer even before this episode.
22. Hunton, 126.

Chapter 8:

1. William Mahone's Recollections, in *Civil War Times Illustrated Collection* (W. G. Briggs Correspondence, 1861-1865), 4. U. S. Army Military History Institute, Carlisle Barracks, PA. Mahone reports this incident as occurring at Amelia Court House, with himself and Major Generals John B. Gordon and Charles W. Field present at the time.
2. *Ibid.*, 126.
3. The full transcript of Lee's March 30, 1865 letter to Early is found in Jubal A. Early, *Autobiographical Sketch and Narrative of the War Between the States* (Wilmington, NC: Broadfoot, 1989 reprint of 1912 edition), 468-69.
4. Hunton, 126-27.
5. Walter H. Taylor to R. E. Cowart of Dallas, TX, November 10, 1908, in Munford-Ellis Papers, MSS Collections, William R. Perkins Library, Duke University, Durham, North Carolina.
6. In *R. E. Lee*, Freeman states that his sources for this story were Colonel Walter Taylor and Major Giles B. Cooke (Vol. IV, 112). The same story is related by John S. Mosby in "Personal Recollections

of General Lee," *Munsey's Magazine*, Vol. 45 (April-September, 1911), 69; and Mosby, *The Memoirs of Colonel John S. Mosby,* ed. by Charles Wells Russell (Boston: Little, Brown, and Co., 1917), 382.

7. *Ibid.*; Regarding historical consensus, see, for instance, Irving P. Whitehead to Judge Daniel Grinnan, May 9, 1931, in MSS Collection, VAHS, Richmond, VA.
8. Harrison, 141-42.
9. Freeman, *R. E. Lee*, Vol. IV, 112; Harrison, 67.
10. Freeman, *Lee's Lieutenants*, Vol. II, 255-56.
11. *Ibid.*, Vol. III, 721.
12. For surrender statistics, see *OR,* XLVI, Pt. 1, 1277f.
13. Freeman and McWhiney, 14.
14. Thomas, 17-18.

Chapter 9:

1. LaSalle Corbell Pickett ("Mrs. General Pickett"), "Personal Memories of Robert E. Lee," *Lippincott's Monthly Magazine*, Vol. LXXIX, January, 1907, 55.
2. *Ibid.*, 57-58.
3. LaSalle Corbell Pickett, *Across My Path: Memories of People I Have Known* (New York: Brentano's, 1916), 96.
4. They did come quite close, however, on at least one occasion. The Lees departed the White Sulphur Springs (Virginia) spa on August 27, 1868, just a few days before the Picketts arrived, thereby perhaps avoiding the clash that occurred when Lee and Pickett met in Richmond in 1870. See Orville Browning, *The Diary of Orville Hickman Browning*, ed. by Theodore C. Pease and James G. Randall (Springfield, IL: Illinois State Historical Library, 1925), Vol. II (1865-1881), 217. For "last sweet memory", see LaSalle Pickett, *Personal Memories of Robert E. Lee*, 58-59.
5. "Disagrees with Colonel Mosby," Richmond *Times-Dispatch*, March 25, 1911, 10.
6. Walter H. Taylor, *Four Years with General Lee*, ed. by James I. Robertson, Jr. (Bloomington: Indiana University Press, 1962), 155; Jefferson Davis, "Jefferson Davis Remembers Robert E. Lee," *The North American Review*, Vol. CL (January, 1890), 65; "Rebel General Pickett," *Executive Doc. No. 11*, House of Representatives, 39th Congress, 2nd Session, 1866-67, Vol. 1288, House Docs., 1-9. Charles Bracelen Flood, *Lee: The Last Years* (Boston: Houghton Mifflin Company, 1981), 44-49.
7. "Virginia wants" quoted in William B. Hesseltine, *Confederate Leaders in the New South* (Baton Rouge: Louisiana State University Press, 1950), 8. Lee and insurance business from Jerrold Northrop Moore, *Confederate Commissary General, Lucius Bellinger Northrop*, (Shippensburg, PA.: White Mane Pub. Co., 1996), 296.

8. In May 1865 Ulysses Grant advised the War Department to offer a reward of $5,000 for Mosby's capture. At about the same time, Ben Butler was agitating for the government to seize Pickett, as it had Jefferson Davis and Henri Wirz, for high crimes against the United States. For Mosby's situation,see Mosby, *Memoirs*, xiii (Introduction).
9. Mosby, *Memoirs*, 381.
10. *Ibid.*
11. From undated clipping, ca., 1911 in George A. Martin Papers (#492) in Southern Historical Collection, University of North Carolina, Chapel Hill, NC. See also Freeman, *R. E. Lee*, Vol. III, 90: "Never in his whole career did [Robert E. Lee] order a general officer under arrest."
12. See Pickett, *The Heart of a Soldier*, 213. This "Editorial Note," like the letters themselves, is what LaSalle Pickett wanted the public to know, and while her heavy-handed editing is reason enough to suspect her account of events, no one knew George Pickett's innermost feelings better than his wife.
13. Richmond *Times-Dispatch*, March 25, 1911, Sec. A, p. 10.
14. *Ibid.*, April 2, 1911, Sec. A, p. 3.
15. Richmond *Daily Whig*, October 21 and November 4, 1870, n.p.
16. Quoted in Richmond *Daily Whig*, "Editorials," October 13, 1870, n.p.
17. Taylor, 156-57.

Chapter 10:

1. Nelson Morehouse Blake, *William Mahone of Virginia: Soldier and Political Insurgent* (Richmond: Garrett & Massie, 1935), 67-68. See also James Stuart Montgomery, *The Shaping of a Battle* (New York: Chilton Company, 1959), 29, 40 ff.
2. Quoted in letter from Horace Lacy to William Mahone, reproduced in Benjamin F. Butler, *Autobiography and Personal Reminiscences of Major-General Benjamin F. Butler; Butler's Book* (Boston: A. M. Thayer & Co., 1892), 881-83.
3. Rod Gragg, "The Quotable Robert E. Lee," *Southern Partisan Magazine*, Fourth Quarter, 1989, 26, 29.
4. At Bristoe Station on October 14, 1863, an impetuous Hill fought arguably the worst battle of his career, getting two of his brigades slaughtered when he sent them into a well-laid trap without first ordering a reconnaissance. After the battle, Lee's only comment was, "Well, well, General, bury these poor men, and let us say no more about it." Robertson, *General A. P. Hill*, 239.
5. Longstreet, *From Manassas to Appomattox*, 332.
6. Freeman, *Lee's Lieutenants*, Vol. II, 666; Dr. Hunter H. McGuire, "Account of the Wounding and Death of Stonewall Jackson," *Richmond Medical Journal*, 1866 (quoted in William J. Miller, ed., "I

Am Badly Injured, Doctor; I Fear I Am Dying," *Civil War Magazine*, Issue No. 56, April, 1996, 55.

7. Margaret Sanborn, *Robert E. Lee: The Complete Man* (New York: J. B. Lippincott, 1967), 146.
8. Quoted in Inman, ed., *Soldier of the South*, 68 and 77. Confirmation of the willingness of Pickett's men to launch another attack immediately is found in Georg and Busey, 186.
9. Quoted by Robert W. Barnwell, "The Battle of Seven Pines," *Confederate Veteran*, ed. by Sumner Cunningham and Edith D. Pope, Vol. XXXVI (1928), 59.
10. A fuller explanation of Lee's hierarchical mindset is contained in Woodworth.
11. Freeman, *Lee's Lieutenants*, Vol. III, 496-97.
12. LaSalle Pickett, *Pickett and His Men*, 425.
13. George B. McClellan to Abraham Lincoln, April 20, 1862, Lincoln Papers, Manuscript Division, Library of Congress, Washington, D.C.
14. Dowdey, 729. Lee apparently considered McClellan "an able but timid commander," according to McClellan's latest biographer. Stephen W. Sears, *George B. McClellan, The Young Napoleon* (New York: Ticknor & Fields, 1988), 273.
15. Late in the war when the Confederates were scrambling to fill their decimated officer ranks, Lee was in constant communication with Jefferson Davis about various officers, including Joseph B. Kershaw, George H. Steuart, John Bell Hood, and William N. Pendleton, to name just a few. See Freeman and McWhiney, viii-ix, xxi-xxii (Introduction), 242, 282, 284.
16. R. E. Lee to Jefferson Davis, November 25, 1862, *OR,* Vol. XXI, 1029-30; Lee to Sec. of War, November 25, 1862, *Ibid.*, 1030; William C. Davis, "Thomas Fenwick Drayton," in *The Confederate General*, Vol. II, 76-77.
17. Freeman and McWhiney, xxi (Introduction).

Selected Bibliography

Manuscript Collections and Unpublished Works

Civil War Times Illustrated Collection. U.S. Army Military History Institute, Carlisle Barracks, Pa.

Cockrell, Monroe F. "Where Was Pickett at Gettysburg?" Typescript (1949) in Alderman Library. University of Virginia. Charlottesville, VA.

John W. Daniel Papers. Special Collections. Alderman Library. University of Virginia. Charlottesville, VA.

Eldridge Collection. Huntington Library. San Marino, CA.

John W. Fairfax Papers, 1863-1937. MSS Collections, Virginia Historical Society. Richmond, VA.

Gordon, Lesley Jill. "Before the Story: The Early Life of George E. Pickett." Honors Thesis submitted for B.A. degree in History. Earl Gregg Swem Library. College of William and Mary. Williamsburg, VA, 1987.

Arthur Crew Inman Papers. Special Collections. John Marshall Library. Brown University. Providence, R.I.

Robert E. Lee Family Papers. MSS Collections. Virginia Historical Society. Richmond, VA.

Robert E. Lee Headquarters Papers, 1850-76. MSS Collections. Virginia Historical Society. Richmond, VA.

Robert E. Lee Papers, University Library, Washington and Lee University. Lexington, VA.

Richard L. Maury Papers. Special Collections. William R. Perkins Library. Duke University. Durham, NC.

Munford-Ellis Papers. MSS Collections. William R. Perkins Library. Duke University. Durham, N.C.

Reardon, Carol Ann. "The Image of 'Pickett's Charge,' 1863-1913: Virginia's Gift to American Martial Tradition." Thesis Submitted for Master of Arts in History, University of South Carolina, 1980.

Southern Historical Collection. Wilson Library. University of North Carolina at Chapel Hill.
George A. Martin Papers
E. P. Alexander Papers
Alexander Cheves Haskell Papers

Gettysburg Newspaper Cuttings Books and Vertical files. Library. Gettysburg National Military Park. Gettysburg, PA.

Primary Sources

Alexander, Porter. *Fighting for the Confederacy*. Gary Gallagher, ed. Chapel Hill: University of North Carolina Press, 1989.

__________. *Military Memoirs of a Confederate: A Critical Narrative*. New York: Charles Scribner's Sons, 1907. Reprint. Indiana University Press, 1962.

Blackford, W.W. *War Years with Jeb Stuart*. New York: Charles Scribner's Sons, 1945.

Browning, Orville. *The Diary of Orville Hickman Browning*. Theodore C. Pease and James G. Randall, eds. 2 vols. Springfield, IL: Illinois State Historical Library, 1925.

Butler, Benjamin F. *Autobiography and Personal Reminiscences of Major-General Benjamin B. Butler; Butler's Book*. Boston: A. M. Thayer & Co., 1892.

Comte de Paris. *The Battle of Gettysburg: From the History of the Civil War in America*. Philadelphia: Porter & Coates, 1886. Reprint. Baltimore: Butternut and Blue Press, 1987.

Conolly, Thomas. *An Irishman in Dixie: Thomas Conolly's Diary of the Fall of the Confederacy*. Nelson D. Lankford, ed. Columbia: University of South Carolina Press, 1988.

Dawson, Francis W. *Reminiscences of Confederate Service, 1861-1865*. 1882. Reprint. Bell I. Wiley, ed. Baton Rouge, LA.: Louisiana State University Press, 1980.

Dooley, John. John Dooley, *Confederate Soldier. His War Journal*. Joseph T. Durkin,ed. New York: Georgetown University Press, 1945.

Dowdey, Clifford, and Louis H. Manarin, eds. *The Wartime Papers of R. E. Lee*. New York: Bramhall, 1961.

Early, Jubal A. Autobiographical Sketch and Narrative of the War Between the States. 1912. Reprint. Wilmington, NC: Broadfoot, 1989.

Fletcher, William A. *Rebel Private: Front and Rear; Memoirs of a Confederate Soldier*. 1908. Reprint. New York: Dutton Books, 1995.

Freeman, Douglas Southall, ed. *Lee's Dispatches: Unpublished Letters of General Robert E. Lee to Jefferson Davis and the War Department, C.S.A., 1862-65*. New York: G.P. Putnam's Sons, 1915.

____________, and Grady McWhiney, eds. *Lee's Dispatches: Unpublished Letters of General Robert E. Lee, C.S.A, to Jefferson Davis, 1862-1865*. rev. ed. New York: G.P. Putnam's Sons, 1957.

Fremantle, Arthur J. L. *Three Months in the Southern States: April-June, 1863*. Edinburgh, Scotland: W. Blackwood and Sons, 1863 Reprint. University of Nebraska Press, 1991.

French, Samuel G. *Two Wars: An Autobiography of General Samuel G. French*. Nashville, TN: Confederate Veteran, 1901.

Geer, Walter. *Campaigns of the Civil War*. New York: Brentano's, 1926.
Gordon, John B. *Reminiscences of the Civil War*. New York: Charles Scribner's Sons, 1904.
Grant, Ulysses. *Memoirs and Selected Letters*. Mary D. and William S. McFeely, eds. Reprint. New York: The Library of America, 1990.
Harrison, Walter. *Pickett's Men: A Fragment of War History*. New York: D. Van Nostrand, 1870. Reprint. Baltimore, MD: Butternut and Blue Press, 1984.
Hood, John Bell. *Advance and Retreat: Personal Experiences in the United States and Confederate States Armies*. New Orleans: Hood Orphan Memorial Fund, 1880. Reprint. Indiana University Press, 1959.
House of Representatives. Executive Document No. 11: "Rebel General Pickett." 39th Congress, 2nd Session, 1866-67. Vol. 1288 House Docs. pp. 1-9.
Hunton, Eppa. *Autobiography*. Richmond: William Byrd Press, 1933.
Johnson, Robert Underwood, and Clarence Clough Buell, eds. *Battles and Leaders of the Civil War*. 4 vols. Based upon *Century Magazine* "War Series," 1884-87. New York: Century Co., 1887-88 Reprint. Castle Books, 1956.
Jones, John B. *A Rebel War Clerk's Diary at the Confederate States Capital*. 2 vols. Philadelphia: J.B. Lippincott and Co., 1866.
___________. *A Rebel War Clerk's Diary*, condensed, edited, and annotated by Earl Schenck Miers. "complete in one volume." New York: Sagamore Press, Inc., 1958.
Kean, Robert G. H. *Inside the Confederate Government: The Diary of Robert Garlick Hill Kean*. Edward Younger, ed. New York: Oxford University Press, 1957.
Long, A. L. *Memoirs of Robert E. Lee: His Military and Personal History*. 1886. Reprint. Secaucus, New Jersey: Castle Books. 1983.
Longstreet, James. *From Manassas to Appomattox: Memoirs of the Civil War in America*. Philadelphia: J.B. Lippincott Co., 1896. Reprint. James I. Robertson, ed. Indiana University Press, 1960.
Marshall, Charles. *An Aide-de-Camp of Lee, Being the Papers of Colonel Charles Marshall, Sometime Aide-de-Camp, Military Secretary, and Assistant Adjutant General on the Staff of Robert E. Lee, 1862-1865*. Frederick Maurice,ed. Boston: Little, Brown and Co., 1927.
McClure, A.K., ed. *The Annals of the War Written by Leading Participants North and South: Originally Published in the Philadelphia Weekly Times*. Philadelphia: Times Publishing Co., 1879. Reprint. Morningside House, 1988.
Mosby, John. *The Memoirs of Colonel John S. Mosby*. Charles Wells Russell, ed. Boston: Little, Brown, and Co., 1917.

Pickett, George E. *The Heart of a Soldier: As Revealed in the Intimate Letters of General George E. Pickett, C.S.A.* LaSalle Pickett, ed. New York: Seth Moyle, Inc., 1913.

_________. *Soldier of the South: General Pickett's War Letters to His Wife.* Arthur Crew Inman, ed. Boston: Houghton Mifflin Company, 1928.

Pickett, LaSalle. *Across My Path: Memories of People I Have Known.* New York: Brentano's, 1916.

_________. *Pickett and His Men.* Atlanta, GA.: The Foote & Davies Co., 1899.

Poague, William T. *Gunner with Stonewall.* Monroe F. Cockrell, ed. Jackson, TN: McCowat-Mercer Press, 1957.

Register of Graduates and Former Cadets of the United States Military Academy, 1802-1948. New York: West Point Alumni Foundation, Inc., 1948.

Scheibert, Justus. *Seven Months in the Rebel States During the North American War, 1863.* Germany, 1875. Translated and reprinted by University of Alabama Press, 1958.

Sheridan, Philip H. *Personal Memoirs of P.H. Sheridan.* 2 vols. New York: D. Appleton and Co., 1888.

Soldier of the Civil War, A. By a member of the Virginia Historical Society. Cleveland, OH: privately printed, 1900. Museum of the Confederacy, Richmond, VA.

Sorrel, G. Moxley. *Recollections of a Confederate Staff Officer.* New York: Neale Publishing Co., 1905. Reprint. Morningside Bookshop, 1978.

Taylor, Walter. *Four Years with General Lee.* New York: D. Appleton and Co., 1877. Reprint. Indiana University Press, 1962.

_________. *General Lee, His Campaigns in Virginia, 1861-65: With Personal Reminiscences.* Norfolk, VA.: Nusbaum, 1906. Reprint. Morningside Bookshop, 1975.

_________. *Lee's Adjutant: The Wartime Letters of Colonel Walter Herron Taylor, 1862-1865.* R. Lockwood Tower, ed., with John S. Belmont. Columbia: University of South Carolina Press, 1995.

U.S. War Department. *The War of the Rebellion: A Compilation of the Official Records of the Union and Confederate Armies.* 70 vols. Washington, D.C.: U.S. Government Printing Office, 1880-1901.

Walker, James H. "Gettysburg." Booklet No. 282 in "Reprints of Original Addresses, Speeches and Documents from Civil War Participants." Suffolk, VA.: Robert Hardy Publications. (privately printed). n.d.

Wright, Marcus J., compiler. *General Officers of the Confederate Army, Officers of the Executive Departments of the Confederate States, Members of the Confederate Congress by States.* New York: Neale Publishing Co., 1911. Reprint. J.M. Carroll and Co., 1983.

Secondary Sources

Barrett, John G. *The Civil War in North Carolina*. Chapel Hill: University of North Carolina Press, 1963.

Blake, Nelson Morehouse. *William Mahone of Virginia: Soldier and Political Insurgent*. Richmond: Garrett & Massie, 1935.

Busey, John W., and David G. Martin. *Regimental Strengths and Losses at Gettysburg*. Hightstown, New Jersey: Longstreet House, 1994.

Cash, W. J. *The Mind of the South*. New York: Alfred A. Knopf, 1965.

Civil War Book of Lists, The. Conshohocken, PA.: Combined Books, 1993.

Coco, Gregory A. *Recollections of a Texas Colonel at Gettysburg*. Gettysburg: Thomas Publications, 1990.

Coddington, Edwin B. *The Gettysburg Campaign: A Study in Command*. Dayton, Ohio: Morningside Bookshop, 1983.

Current, Richard N., ed. *Encyclopedia of the Confederacy*. 4 vols. New York: Simon & Schuster, 1993.

Davis, Burke. *To Appomattox: Nine April Days, 1865*. Reprint. Washington, DC: Eastern Acorn Press, 1981.

Davis, William C., ed. *The Confederate General*. 6 vols. Harrisburg, PA.: National Historical Society, 1991.

Dowdey, Clifford. *Lee*. Boston: Little, Brown and Company, 1965.

________. *Lee's Last Campaign*. Boston: Little Brown & Co., 1960.

Dufour, Charles L. *The Mexican War: A Compact History, 1846-1848*. New York: Hawthorn Books, 1968.

Eisenschiml, Otto, and E.B. Long. *As Luck Would Have It; Chance and Coincidence in the Civil War*. Indianapolis: Bobbs-Merrill, 1948.

Flood, Charles Bracelen. *Lee: The Last Years*. Boston: Houghton Mifflin Co., 1981.

Freeman, Douglas Southall. *Lee's Lieutenants: A Study in Command*. 3 vols. New York: Charles Scribner's Sons, 1942, 1944.

________. *R.E. Lee: A Biography*. 4 vols. New York: Charles Scribner's Sons, 1935.

Georg, Kathleen, and John W. Busey. *Nothing But Glory: Pickett's Division at Gettysburg*. Hightstown, New Jersey: Longstreet House, 1987.

Glatthaar, Joseph T. *Partners in Command*. New York: The Free Press, 1994.

Griffith, Paddy. *Battle Tactics of the Civil War*. New Haven: Yale University Press, 1989.

Hartje, Robert G. *Van Dorn: The Life and Times of a Confederate General*. Nashville, TN.: Vanderbilt University Press, 1967.

Hesseltime, William B. *Confederate Leaders in the New South*. Baton Rouge: Louisiana State University Press, 1950.

Longstreet, Helen D. *Lee and Longstreet at High Tide: Gettysburg in the Light of the Official Records*. Gainesville: GA: published by author, 1904. Reprint. Broadfoot, 1988.
Lykes, Richard Wayne. *The Campaign for Petersburg*. Washington, DC: National Park Service, n.d.
McKim, Randolph H. *The Soul of Lee*. New York: Longmans, Green and Co., 1918.
Miers, Earl Schenck, and Richard Brown, eds. *Gettysburg*. New Brunswick, New Jersey: Rutgers University Press, 1948.
Montgomery, James Stuart. *The Shaping of a Battle*. New York: Chilton Company, 1959.
Moore, Jerrold Northrop. *Confederate Commissary General, Lucius Bellinger Northrop*. Shippensburg, PA.: White Mane Pub. Co., 1996.
Murfin, James V. *The Gleam of Bayonets*. Cranbury, New Jersey: Thomas Yoseloff, 1965.
Robertson, James I., Jr. *General A. P. Hill*. New York: Random House, 1987.
Sanborn, Margaret. *Robert E. Lee: The Complete Man*. New York: J. B. Lippincott, 1967.
Sears, Stephen W. *George B. McClellan, The Young Napoleon*. New York: Ticknor & Fields, 1988.
Taylor, Emerson Gifford. *Gouverneur Kemble Warren: Life and Letters of an American Soldier*. 1933. Reprint. Gaithersburg, MD.: Ron Van Sickle Military Books, 1988.
Thomas, Emory. *Robert E. Lee, A Biography*. New York: W. W. Norton & Co., 1995.
Tucker, Glenn. *Lee and Longstreet at Gettysburg*. Indianapolis, IN: Bobbs-Merrill, 1968.
Wector, Dixon. *The Hero in America: A Chronicle of Hero Worship*. New York: Charles Scribner's Sons, 1941.
Wert, Jeffrey. *General James Longstreet*. New York: Simon & Schuster, 1993.
Woodworth, Steven E. *Davis and Lee at War*. Lawrence, KS: University Press of Kansas, 1995.
Young, William A., and Patricia C. Young. *56th Virginia Infantry*. Virginia Regimental History Series. Lynchburg, VA.: H.E. Howard, 1990.

Periodicals and Anthologies

Bauer, Daniel. "'The Most Conspicuous Failure': The Slaughter of the North Carolina Brigade on Gettysburg's First Day," *CIVIL WAR Magazine*. Vol. XVII. 1989. 7-14.
Brown, Kent Masterson. "Lee at Gettysburg: The Man, the Myth, the Recriminations." *CIVIL WAR Magazine*. Vol. XI, No. 1, Issue 39 (January - February, 1993). 8-14 ff.

Cunningham, Sumner, and Edith D. Pope, eds. *Confederate Veteran.* 40 vols. Nashville, TN.: S. A. Cunningham, 1893-1932.

Davis, Jefferson. "Jefferson Davis Remembers Robert E. Lee," *The North American Review*. Vol. CL (January, 1890). 55-66.

Early, Jubal, J. William Jones, et al, eds. *Southern Historical Society Papers*. Richmond: Southern Historical Society, 1876-1959. 52 vols. plus index. Reprint. 1977-80.

Freehoff, William F., compiler. "Southern Sampler." *Southern Partisan Magazine*. 2nd Quarter, 1996. 43.

Goethels, Gregor. "Sacred-Secular Icons," *Icons of America*. Ray Browne and Marshall Fishwick, eds. Bowling Green, OH: Bowling Green State University Popular Press, 1978.

Gragg, Rod. "The Quotable Robert E. Lee," *Southern Partisan Magazine*. Fourth Quarter, 1989. 25-31.

Holsworth, Jerry W. "Uncommon Valor: Hood's Texas Brigade in the Maryland Campaign." *Blue & Gray Magazine*. Vol. XIII, No. 6. August, 1996. 6-20 ff.

Marsden, Michael T. "Iconology of the Western Romance," *Icons of America*. Ray Browne and Marshall Fishwick, eds. Bowling Green, OH: Bowling Green State University Popular Press, 1978.

Miller, William J., ed. "I Am Badly Injured, Doctor; I Fear I Am Dying." *CIVIL WAR Magazine*. Issue No. 56, April, 1996. 52-58.

Mosby, John S. "Personal Recollections of General Lee," *Munsey's Magazine*. Vol. 45, No. 1 (April, 1911). 65-69.

Nachbar, Jack, and Kevin Lause. "Living in the Material World: The Meaning and Power of Popular Icons," *Popular Culture: An Introductory Text*. Nachbar and Lause, eds. Bowling Green, OH: Bowling Green State University Popular Press, 1994.

Philadelphia *Weekly Times*. 1885.

Pickett, Mrs. General George E. "The Wartime Story of General Pickett." *Cosmopolitan Magazine*. Vol. LVI, No. 1. December, 1913. 33-42.

Reardon, Carol. "Pickett's Charge: The Convergence of History and Myth in the Southern Past," in *Third Day at Gettysburg and Beyond*. Gary Gallagher, ed. Chapel Hill: University of North Carolina Press, 1994.

Richmond *Times-Dispatch*, 1903, 1904, 1911.

Smith, Everand H., ed. "As They Saw General Lee," *Civil War Times Illustrated*. Vol. XXV, No. 6. October, 1986. 20-23.

Williams, H. David. "The Glory of War: Johnny Reb and the Antietam Campaign," *Virginia Country's Civil War Quarterly* (now known as *CIVIL WAR Magazine*). Vol. IX. 1987. 13-25.

Wood, W.W. "Pickett's Charge at Gettysburg," Philadelphia *Times*. August 11, 1877.

Index

About the Author

Richard F. Selcer received his BA and MA degrees from Austin College in Sherman, Texas, and his Ph.D from Texas Christian University. Ever since he "bumped into" the legend that is George E. Pickett, his fascination with one of the most complex figures of the Civil War has grown. A professor of history at the International Christian University and Dallas County Community College, Dr. Selcer is also the author of several other works, *Hell's Half Acre: The Life and Legend of a Red-Light District*; *The Fort That Became a City: An Illustrated History of Fort Worth*; and *"Faithfully and Forever Your Soldier"—General George E. Pickett.*